Apparently, God Needed a Drummer

By

Tammy Fleming

Sharlotte — Congratulations! Best of Luck in your Future endeavors! Tammy Box (Fleming)

ISBN 13: 978-0-9823972-2-0
ISBN 10: 0-9823972-2-0

© 2009

Dedicated to Erin, Tommy, and Joey.
May you always remember to
appreciate the things in life most
of us take for granted every day.

Acknowledgements...................

I would like to thank everyone who contributed to the stories in this book. Your love for Jason made his life so full and meaningful. He loved each and every one of you, and I am so glad he had you all in his life.

I would also like to thank Andy Box for his help with everything I needed to get the book ready for the printer. His expertise and creative input turned my idea into a completed project that I am proud of.

My parents, my sister and brothers and their families continue to give me strength and support by keeping the JCW Scholarship Fund growing and providing support to those who need it. They help me keep Jason's memory and spirit alive every day.

And, finally, thanks to Dick Marchesani, for professionally editing and proofing. Our longtime friendship allowed him to keep it genuine and real for me.

The last week he was in the hospital, I went down to the CT Scan Lab with Jason before a test. We were both in good spirits and joking around. Looking back, I realize now that he was on some pretty good drugs, and I was probably punchy-exhausted, but we were laughing and being silly. While waiting for the CT I noticed that he had an eyelash on his cheek. I took it, held it up to him, and told him to make a wish and blow. He opened his mouth wide and pretended to breathe out hard. I laughed and said, "C'mon, make a wish!" Again he pretended to blow, and nothing came out. Finally, he took the oxygen hose out of his nose, and held it up to the lash. We cracked up!

We had talked before about writing a book about the experience of dealing with cancer, and his struggles, the stupid things that we did to cope with it. I mentioned it again while we were waiting in that hall. I said he would have to help me remember, because over the previous five years, it seemed that my mind was so full of worry and fear, that there were many things that just escaped the "memory" section of my brain, unless someone reminded me. Even then, I still don't remember a lot of details of every day life during that time. So, that was the plan.

That was on Thursday, May 22, 2008. He passed away on Tuesday, May 27, 2008, at the age of 25, one day short of his 5 year anniversary of being diagnosed with liver cancer. Although, the Camden boys decided since it was a leap year, he technically made it.

I didn't think about writing again, until several months later. I knew I couldn't do him justice if I tried to write without his input - his sense of humor, his memory, his strength, his point of view. It would just end up being like the journal I should have kept for the five years, but didn't. And then I had an idea. I asked everyone who

4

knew him who wanted to contribute, to send me stories about Jason. Funny stories, stories that showed his character (and what a CHARACTER), stories that made them remember him as their brother, friend, nephew, cousin, grandson, mentor, or whatever role he played in their lives. I would take them, and the emails I could come up with, and some things he had on his MySpace page, and put something together.

Now, the morning I had come up with this idea, I called my mother, and sent an email to my sister to bounce the idea off of them. My mother said it would be hard, and I think now couldn't talk about the whole thing. I think my sister thought it was a good idea. I hadn't told anyone else about it yet. But, what was amazing is that same day, unsolicited and completely out of the blue, I received an email from Bob Scales. (Bob was a good friend of Jason's, and happened by chance to be at our house the day he passed away.) Bob had never emailed me in my life that I could remember, and for him to send me this story, on that day, convinced me that Jason must have thought the book was a good idea as well.

This is the email Bob sent:

> *Dear Tammy,*
>   *I hope you are doing well. I didn't get a chance to say bye and thank you the other day at the memorial, so thank you very much for setting up that service at the cemetery; it was great to see all of those loved ones giving support to each other. I think that this scholarship fund is an amazing chance to really keep the torch that Jay lit alive and well. Whether the fund is used for scholarships to students or donated to a cause that fights cancer or helps those afflicted with it, it is*

*something that Jay wanted to do for a long time.
He and I spoke about it about three months before
he left us. So the first part of this letter is to offer
my unyielding support to you and your family and
Jay's foundation. Hopefully you already knew
that but just in case I wanted to put it out there.*

*The second part of this letter is to tell you a
story that played out today that simply amazed me,
and completely filled me with appreciation and
gratitude for everything that Jay and I had done
while he was with us. I will try to keep this as to
the point as possible but I do have a tendency to
wander and digress while writing, so bear with me.*

*As you know, Jay and I did quite a bit of
hunting over the past 7 or 8 years or so; and they
are some of my fondest memories – not just of Jay
but of my life. Chrissy and I helped Jay last year
when he wanted to own his own rifle. I know you
weren't a big fan of it, but it was something that
he really enjoyed and looked forward to doing. He
told me about this rifle that he found. It was a
really good deal and Chrissy and I decided to buy
it for him. He insisted on paying us back but after
about a week of arguing with him I convinced him
to accept it as a gift, with the promise that he
would hunt with me as often as he could.*

*Jay and I hunted hard last year during
deer season; he was feeling well enough then to
walk pretty far distances and we really went out
there and worked hard. I was determined to get
him into a position to get a deer. Regretfully, I
was not able to. We still hunted though, and had a
great time just being out there and in each others*

company. A couple of months before the doctors found the tumors in his lungs he really wanted to go hunting, but he could not walk very far without going into the fits of breathing difficulties that he went into. I planned it out for a couple of days and ended up figuring a way, (by truck and four wheeler) to get him to a place where he had a great chance to see a deer. It never panned out, but we sat out there for hours and just before we packed it up to leave, he said that he would like to shoot the rifle. I set up a can target and paced it out for him and he took a couple of shots.

On the way back to my house that night he said that he probably would not be able to hunt again for a while because the cold was bothering his lungs. He asked me to take his rifle with me when I hunted. He essentially said that if he wasn't able to get a deer with it that year, that he at least wanted the rifle to get a deer. I thought it was a perfect Jay thing to say and told him that I would do what I could. I did not get another deer that year.

After he gave me the rifle, I was hell bent on getting that deer with it and have been hunting nearly every day since the opening of deer season about a month and a half ago. I was having a really hard time hunting because it didn't feel right without Jay there, and it made my heart ache to not have him there. I considered giving up hunting for good because I just thought it would never be the same without him, and it won't.

Today I was dragged out by a mutual friend Jay and I shared, Mike Pounds. We hunted

7

again all day, me with Jay's rifle, and saw
nothing.   I had not been to the place where Jay
and I last hunted since that day he and I were
there the previous season.   I was very hesitant to
go there today, but I decided that Jay would
probably kick my ass and tell me to go if he knew
about me avoiding that place.

In the very last moments of our hunt today
a little bit before 1:00pm, I was walking through
the woods trying to hunt but mostly thinking about
Jay - (I often have little conversations with him in
my head as if he were still there. Hopefully that
doesn't make me weird. I don't think it does.)-
when a slight movement caught my eye.   It took
me about a half an hour, but I was able to creep
up within a couple of hundred yards of a deer and
I finally succeeded in fulfilling my promise to Jay
by taking a deer with his rifle.

After the shot I rushed towards the deer out of
sheer excitement and managed to lose track of
where it was when I shot it.   I started panicking
thinking that I may have missed it, or that I only
wounded it and it ran off, which Jay and I agreed
would be awful.   After about 15 minutes of
walking around, something shiny caught my eye
on the ground about 10 yards in front of me. I
walked over to it and about five yards from this
shiny object was the deer.   It was a huge eight
point buck, the nicest deer I have ever shot. I
returned to the shiny object to see what it was and
was almost forced to my knees from emotion when
I realized that it was the shell casing from the last
shot that Jay fired from his rifle. I had, without
being aware of it, walked over three miles in and

around these woods, back and forth, and ended up taking this deer with his rifle at the exact spot where he and I had last hunted.

I think that Jay would be very pleased with the way that it all worked out. He always saw the meaning in small things like that, but that to me is no small thing. I will remember that for the rest of my life. It will be a story that I will tell my grandchildren, I am sure.

I am sorry for dragging on with the story, and I hope that you enjoyed it even though I don't think hunting is one of your favorite subjects. Thank you again Tammy for everything; you raised Jay and he was my best friend. It is because of you that he became the man that he was, and that man was at an equal level of importance and occupied the same space in my heart as my wife and family. So again, I thank you for that.

I hope to talk to you again soon.

Love
Bob

I sat and stared at this email and thought, "Are you kidding me?" It was **exactly** what I was thinking about for this book. I knew there were hundreds of stories out there, and I just had to tap into them!

So, that's what I am going to try to do.

This is it:

In May, 2003, we moved into a new house, the first one I ever bought. After struggling for years, living paycheck to paycheck, and dodging bill collectors, I was finally in a place where I felt good about our family emotionally, financially, and stability-wise. Andy Box and I had a great relationship. We had been together for three years, and it had been a tough time. My divorce from Bob Fleming had not been easy on my three sons, Jason, Tommy, and Joey; and I was hoping that the move would give us a new start together as a family. Tommy and Joey were adjusting well to that and the move to Rome, and Jason was starting to be more responsible. His relationship with Andy was also coming around, slowly but surely. We were all excited about the new house, and had plans to remodel and really make it our own.

Around the third week of May, Jason was complaining about having a stomach ache. Pretty low key, I thought, nothing to worry about. After about the third day of him telling me about it, I decided to make him an appointment with the doctor just to make sure it wasn't serious. My actual thought was "Ok, I better get him checked because if he has appendicitis or something, I will feel really bad if it ruptures!"

I called our doctor, and he was out. So, I had to make an appointment with the doctor who was covering, Barbara Connor. Luckily, she was an internist, and she was able to get us right in that day. When she examined Jason, she said it didn't seem like his appendix because of where the pain was. She ordered a blood test, and when it came back, she said she wanted him to have a sonogram just to check things out. I wasn't worried. I knew her, trusted her, and Jay had never had a cavity, or broke a bone, or was barely ever even sick in his whole 20 years.

The next day, I sent him by himself to the hospital to have the sonogram done. I went to work like it was a normal day. He called me and said they did the sonogram, and the girl left the room and then came back in and said she had talked to the doctor, and she wanted him to come back the next day for a CT Scan. Ok, you have my attention now.

I don't remember the events of those first few days exactly, but I know I called our regular doctor, David Kirk, who I trusted with my life. He had delivered my other two boys, Tommy and Joey, and had been our family doctor for almost 10 years. I asked him if he had talked to Dr. Connor, and he said he had, but he didn't know anything until the CT was done. So, we had the CT Scan and waited for him to call. When he finally called, I could tell by his tone he was worried. He said there was a "mass" on Jason's liver. (Mass?) He said we had to have a biopsy done on the following Monday. (Biopsy?) Oh, ok, no problem. And I really don't remember waiting until Monday. I am not sure what we talked about that weekend, or what we were thinking. I don't remember anything but maybe thinking it must be a mistake.

That Monday we went for the biopsy. My mother was with me, and we just sat outside the room waiting. When they were done, and they brought him to recovery, we asked the radiologist for his opinion, and he said there was something there, and it didn't look good. We would have to wait for the lab results.

The next day, May 28th, 2003, I went to work, and waited for the call. Dr. Kirk called me and said he had the results.

"What is it?" I said.

12

"Fibrolamellar Hepatocellular Carcinoma."
Carcinoma. I got that part. "Spell it." I wrote the name down on one of my business cards.

Liver cancer. A very rare form of liver cancer. Oh my God.

I left work, got in my car and called my mother. My father answered. She wasn't home - I had to tell him. Oh, God. "It's CANCER, dad!" By now I was crying hysterically.

He asked if I wanted him to come get me, but I said no. I had to try to process this. I needed some time. I called Andy and told him the news, and asked him to meet me at home to tell Jay. I called my sister. My brother-in-law answered and told me she was in the bathroom crying. My father had called her.

When I got home, Andy was there and my parents had just pulled up. We stood out back, hugged, I think, and then went inside. Jason was in his room. I called him out to the kitchen and handed him the business card. "What's this?" he asked.

"That's what you have. It's a rare form of liver cancer." Things get a little fuzzy immediately after that. I know my family all came over that night. I don't remember much more specifically about that night.

The next day we went to Dr. Kirk's office, and he had set us up with a referral to Strong Memorial Hospital in Rochester, NY. They have a liver transplant department that few can rival. He also told us that Dr. Connor had caught the problem through his blood test. He said there was a number for his liver function that was "slightly" elevated. He said it was so slight, that he may not have caught it if he had done the test. We felt lucky. Isn't that strange?

So, that was it. He had cancer. I had no idea what to do. Even though we knew several people who had cancer, mostly from Camden, we had never really had to deal with it head on. The following week was the Relay For Life in Camden. As Jason says, I dragged him down there to see what it was all about, because it had something to do with cancer, and he had cancer. It turned out to be one of the most moving things I had ever experienced. Jason and I split up when we got there and we were just talking to people we knew, filling in the blanks for everyone about his diagnosis, and what was going on. I couldn't believe the number of people there that we knew. It seemed to have touched someone from every family in town. It was during the luminary ceremony that it must have hit both of us and we frantically searched the crowd for each other. He ran up to me and we just stood there hugging each other, crying.

Deb Harlander was very active in the Camden ACS Relay for Life chapter, and her sons, Ryan and Mark, were very close to Jason. I asked her to send me her memories of Jason, and specifically his Relay connection.

To say that Jay was like one of my own children seems at times selfish. I think that one of Jay's gifts on this earth was being able to adapt to whoever he was with, and accept them for who they were. I met Jay when he was very young. He was my son Ryan's best friend. Ryan was very shy and didn't have a lot of close friends, but Jay was one of them. Through the years he became good friends with both of my sons. I think at times it was Jay and the boys' mission to make me laugh until I either cried or wet my pants. They were relentless in their mission, and I cherish every moment. Jay and I shared laughter and tears through the years, and as he grew up, I not only thought of myself as Mama H, but his friend. I was blessed that his mother shared him with me, and so thankful to this day that Jay was placed in my life.

When Jay was diagnosed with cancer in 2003, I didn't want to believe it. The boys kept telling me, but I had to hear it from Jay. When we held Camden's second American Cancer Society Relay for Life, and I saw Jay and his family at the field that hot June day, I just knew it was true. Jay just came to me, sat me down and told me everything. When I cried, his strength wrapped around me and he told me he would fight this thing, and he was going to win. I believed him and at that moment I began sending him my strength. As the evening came, Jay and his family saw the love of our community poured out on him when the luminaries were lit. It seemed like hundreds of bags had his name on it to honor him. I think in my heart this strengthened him.

That first year after his diagnosis Jay went through so much - surgeries, chemo, radiation, you name it; and they threw it at him. But it was that year that Jay and his friends put together Team Triumph. Jay was the guest speaker at Relay that year and he lit the torch to start the luminary ceremony. He was physically weak, but so strong at the same time. I was going to be taking over as chairperson for the Relay the next year, and Jay promised to be on the planning committee.

The next six months Jay was still going through his treatments, but when we held our first planning meeting, Jay was there. Kathy Peters, our ACS Community Director, was at the meeting. Jay sat there and listened as we talked about how we wanted to go about planning the next Relay. Then Jay spoke up and said, "I have some questions. I want to know, line by line, how much we spent to put on this event last year." Kathy was prepared, and gave him the breakdown. Jay told us, and I believe it became my mission, "We need to get out there and get as much of this logistical stuff for free. Every penny that we spend on putting on this event is less money that goes to cancer research." He was absolutely right. He made it his mission to have a great event, and to include the entire community in the event. He knew it cost money to put on an event like this, but he made sure we were conscious of every penny we spent. That year we got our entertainment tent for free, we had volunteers for concessions, companies donated water, and I believe we came in at or under our budget that was set for us by ACS. That year at Relay, Tammy came up to me, hugged me and told me that this event was part of why Jay fights so hard. Those words as a mother held me in her arms, comforting me in my selfish anger at this disease, made me even more determined to wipe out cancer.

The following year, Jay was by my side again in the planning, but asked if our teams could merge as he was pretty busy with his band and life. We became Triumphant Survivor that year. It was freezing cold that year, (like 40 degrees) and it rained the entire day, but Jay was there with his band, tired but ever present.

In 2008, our sixth Relay and my third and final year as chairperson, Jay was fighting a raging battle. When I saw him just before Christmas in a parking lot at Walmart, I helped him with his bags and we sat in his van and talked for an hour. He told me that he was pretty sick, but he wasn't giving up. We talked about so much that day, but most of all I will always remember how much he loved me. That time I had with Jay was a gift from God, as we never had another chance to talk like that again. We cried some and we laughed a lot, because even through all of his pain, he could still make me smile.

Jay passed away on my 30th Wedding Anniversary, May 27, 2008. Two weeks later at our Relay for Life we paid tribute to Jay, who had worked so hard to fight cancer. I knew he was there in so many ways, but mostly, I could hear him in my ear saying, "Remember Deb, every penny that is spent on this event, is less money that goes to research."

I will miss you and love you forever Jay, and I will continue the fight for you and my family, who continues their fight against cancer.

*****

They got us in very quickly at Strong Memorial Hospital. Within a few days, we were in Rochester, in a hotel, and he was getting tested and poked and prodded every which way at the hospital. We met with the surgeon, Dr. Mark Orloff, and there was more bad news. They couldn't operate on the tumor because it was too big, and a liver transplant was out, because the cancer had spread to the lymph nodes outside his liver. Luckily, it hadn't gone further, but we would have to talk to the oncologist and do chemotherapy first.

His chief oncologist's name was Dr. Alok Khorana. Strong was a teaching hospital, and he was a researcher. We liked him immediately, and we felt very confident in his ability to fix Jason. He explained to us that he would do several rounds of chemotherapy with four different medicines (PIAF) on a 21 day cycle. The PIAF stood for Cisplatin, Interferon, Adreamiacin, and 5FU. He would go into the hospital and have the treatments for four days at a time, then one day of just fluids, to wash it out of his system. Then have three weeks off in between to "recover". He also had Neulasta shots after each cycle to help rebuild his white blood cells. Then, the cycle was repeated. Once the tumor was reduced enough, they could do the surgery.

The staff at the hospital was absolutely fantastic. They were caring and patient - (and young and pretty). Because he was only 20 at the time he was diagnosed, he was always the youngest person on the floor. He was just over the "child" age of 18, or he would have been put on the pediatric oncology floor, and he would have probably been the oldest. So, being the youngest, he would flirt with the younger nurses, be spoiled by the older nurses, and hang with the male nurses. He had it made as far as getting the best care while he was in the hospital.

They were very good to me as well. I could stay with Jay as long as I wanted (or as long as we could stand each other, as the case sometimes was). There was a place nearby called Hope Lodge that was sponsored by the American Cancer Society. People needing a place to stay could stay there for free while their family member was getting treatment at one of the local hospitals. They had a community kitchen, several living areas, a library, and dorm-like rooms. It was clean and comfortable, and a godsend because I wouldn't have been able to afford to stay at the local hotels for as many visits as we ended up needing.

He had to stay in the hospital for five or six days for each chemo session. He would have the first chemo treatment on Monday night, and for the next three days, they would administer the "medicine" through his IV, while giving him fluids to flush it out of his system. I remember vividly the first time they came in to start the treatment. It was so scary for me, but Jason was fascinated with the whole thing. He wanted to know what each drug was, why they were giving him that, and what they expected it to do. The nurses had to wear these big blue gowns and gloves and eyewear, because the medicine was so strong and dangerous. All I could think of was that they were putting this stuff in him that would kill not only (hopefully) the cancer but the good cells, too. It was all surreal to me. I had to walk out of the room when they first started because I couldn't watch.

We didn't know what to expect with the chemo since there were several side effects, and everyone responded differently. Usually, they said, it took a day or so for the symptoms to appear, so we basically just waited. The second day, he would get achy from the Interferon. The other symptoms would show up later in the cycle.

In hind sight, that first cycle wasn't that bad for Jason. He seemed to bounce back quicker than we expected, and I felt a false sense of relief. Maybe this wouldn't be so bad. Of course, that was nothing more than wishful thinking. As the cycles went on, the recovery was longer and longer. They gave him nausea meds that helped, but didn't take it away completely. He would have pain in his joints from the Interferon, I think, and was totally exhausted for the first week when he got home. He would start to feel better the second week, and by the third week, he was almost back to normal. Then, he had to go back and do it again. It was very hard on him, but he was a trooper most of the time. He rarely complained about it.

Jason had several friends that were still in school at the time, and some of them were in the Rochester area attending college. Since Rochester was about two hours from Rome, it was hard for people to just stop in and visit. But almost every week that he was out there, some of the kids would make the trip out to see him. They were such a close group in school and growing up in the small town of Camden, that Jason's illness devastated his friends. But even though he was the one who was sick, and going through all that he was, they still came to him for advice and guidance. He would help them solve their problems, and they would cry on his shoulder. His friend Kathy Wright said that Jason had once told her he was glad it was him who was sick and not one of his friends; because he knew he could handle it.

This is his profile on his MySpace page.

Alright, long story short...

My name's Jay. I play drums in my rock band The

Blueprint. We're good. I have cancer. Every day I die a little, but I live a little more. I like to drink but a lot of times can't. I am a social butterfly. I live in Utica in my buddy's basement. 93% of my ex girlfriends still like me. I always have the best comebacks, 5 minutes after the conversation ends. I like when Nick's mom cooks dinner. It's good. And it's free. I'm convinced that this band is supposed to make it in music. I'm also aware of the chances of failure. Adam Nolan's chances of failure were about 99%. So what's really good?

I've had sex in the McDonalds parking lot. That girl then ran off with one of my best friends and from what I hear they're very happy together. I'm getting a tattoo next week. "Next week" refers to the next week that I have money to spend on getting a tattoo. It's gonna have a lot of personal meaning because I f**** hate when people pick their tattoos out of a tattoo book that's sitting on the counter of the tattoo parlor. Express yourself.

My band gets progressively further along every day. We're doing things we can't talk about. I guess you could call us the Secret Agents of rock and roll. On second thought, please don't.

Deep Thoughts by Jack Handey changed my life. Deep Thoughts by Mark, however, are just usually a drug induced string of nonsensical words, pasted together with bong resin. Crazy kid.

I miss high school. Kids who say they can't wait to get outta high school are crazy. I used to wake up every day, go hang out with two or three hundred of my closest friends, eat lunch for a dollar and ten cents, play sports and other than that, not do a hell of a lot. And plus I was way more attractive back then.

I want to live in California, just to see what its like.

I wish I knew karate. I would use it in all the wrong ways. I wish I knew how to play piano. I would use it for all the wrong reasons. Steve Anderson is my friend and for every reason I can think of, shouldn't be. Kevin is the quarterback and I catch touchdowns. If you meet me, chances are the first thing I'll do is flip you off. Don't take it personal. I have half a liver. I work at Hannaford. I sell lotto tickets and cigarettes to people who should be buying food for their kids. Does that make me a bad person? Cause if not, I got some more for ya, just ask. Loon from Matchmaker is my idol. My American Idol. My Billy Idol. But NOT my Idol Hands. That is something completely different. I wish I was better at the drums. But I'm better than Ringo Starr and he did pretty good.

I listen to Rap Music sometimes, when I can get away with it. I don't keep in touch with my friends from home as much as I should. I feel bad about that. I do miss everyone though. I don't have a car, and I don't make very much money. I skate by on charm and routine haircuts.

If getting in a girl's brain was as easy as getting in her pants, guys would get along with girls a lot more. Girls are from Pluto. And they have cooties.

I will read every single MySpace bulletin from

"Bulls On Parade". I don't even know that kid's real name, but he's real interesting.

My favorite song of all time is "Owner of a Lonely Heart" by YES.

"Owner of a Lonely Heart".....who would have known?

I think this captures a lot of his personality, but not quite the depth of his heart. Everyone who knew him - loved him. I mean, truly loved him. And he loved everyone. I remember one year we were going from Camden to Rome on Thanksgiving Day. It was pretty bad weather, and the roads were slick. We passed a car that had obviously gone off the road and slammed into a snow bank. There was no one around when we passed. Jason saw the car and he said something about the people probably going on their way to Thanksgiving dinner, like we were, and how sad it was that they went off the road. A minute or two later, I heard sniffling. I looked back, and he was crying. He was probably about 9 or 10 at the time. That was the depth of his heart - even at that age.

One of the people we met at Strong who became a good friend was Lisa McNiece. She was the "New Patient Coordinator" for the James P. Wilmont Cancer Center at the hospital. However, no matter what we did, or needed throughout the five years, she was the one who we went to.

Jason had little tolerance for people who did not do their jobs properly. And, unfortunately, he had a knack for attracting people who did NOT do their jobs properly, and it infuriated him. Lisa was one of the few people who gained his respect simply by doing her job - actually going above and beyond her "job" and really taking care of him

23

(and me) at times. I remember one time he called her after not seeing or talking to her in several months. She answered the phone, and he said "Hi, is this Lisa?" and she said, "Yes! Is this Jason?" She recognized his voice after all that time, and all the patients she takes care of on a daily basis. She has a MySpace page, and listed Jay as her "hero" on it.

Here is the post:

"Jason Wilhelm (RIP)5/27/08 is my hero. I have never known someone so strong, brave and enduring. One of the most talented people, I miss you and will never forget you. You made what I do everyday worth each and every bit of effort. I love you J. "

For someone in her position - someone who deals with cancer patients every day on every level - to have that strong an emotional bond with my son really made me proud of him. He impacted so many lives with the same deep, emotional, passionate connection that I never truly realized until he was gone. He made everyone feel as though they were his best friend, and I know he believed they each were.

So we went to the hospital every month and did what he was supposed to do. They would do CT Scans every three months to see how the tumor was responding to the treatment. It was shrinking, but not quite fast enough. I would try to think of things to keep him occupied in the hospital to keep his spirits up, make sure he kept his appetite up, and to keep his mind off of what we were doing there.

I remember one time, my mother was with us, and

we saw a commercial for Red Lobster, or maybe a local seafood place with lobster. Jason said, "Oooh, Lobster!" That was it. It was such a challenge to get him to want to eat during those times in the hospital, that we would try anything. Mom and I went to Wegman's and bought all this stuff - Lobster, potatoes, rolls, desert, a whole dinner and then some. It probably cost about $60 by the time we were finished with the silly details. We went back to the Hope Lodge, and steamed the lobster, (stunk up the place with the fish smell - I felt bad!) baked the potatoes, packed it all up in foil, and brought it to the hospital.

The nurses were all amazed with the whole ordeal. We walked into Jay's room with the meal, and I think the smell of everything almost made him throw up. Of course, he didn't say that right away. He let us spread it all out, and set it up for him, and he tried. Really. Then he just looked at me and said, "Mom, I'm sorry, I can't!" Honestly, I was more upset that he couldn't eat anything than anything else. But the funniest thing was that at about the same time, the commercial came on again for the lobster dinner at the restaurant that started the whole foolish thing. Entire lobster dinner for $19.99 - no cooking, no mess, no smell! We are idiots!

*****

By October, he had already had six rounds of chemo, and Dr. Khorana wanted Dr. Orloff to do the surgery, because there was a limit to how much chemo he could have without it doing more damage than good, long term. I think at that point, eight was the limit they were comfortable with. Dr. Orloff said he couldn't do the surgery because the tumor was still too big, and he wouldn't be able to get it all. I felt like they just kept passing him back and forth to each other. It was the first

25

time since he was diagnosed that I was really afraid because they didn't know what to do at that point. Up until then, we had a plan, they were confident; they knew what they were doing.

I remember calling my sister from the hospital and telling her that they didn't know what to do next. Sometimes it was so hard being out there alone with him. We would get on each other's nerves because we were just too close to each other, and the situation. I felt like it was my job to take care of him, and like I was supposed to know what to do in every situation, and I just didn't. When the doctors were at a standoff, I remember I had a meltdown after I talked to my sister. But, I went back to his room and had to try to stay as level as possible so I wouldn't upset him.

We soon learned that we couldn't predict when the bad news would strike. In the mean time, we had to just wait for something to happen and go through the motions. I am not sure how much of that situation Jason actually realized. He would rarely let on when he was scared or worried about anything. He would do everything in his power to let everyone know that he was "OK" and staying positive, under any circumstances.

It was that same month that our family and friends got together and gave us a benefit to raise money for the expenses of Jason's treatments and the hospital stays. My employer had been very generous by giving me the time off to go and stay with Jason during his hospital stays. They even paid for our hotel room the first time we went to Rochester for his testing. I remember we went to check into the hotel with my parents, and the girl telling me the rooms were taken care of already. I didn't understand who would do that, or who even knew where we were staying.

She said, "Your employer called and took care of it." For the first few months, they even paid me for the time I missed, but after that, I had to take the time without pay.

The benefit was amazing. There is something to be said for the small town of Camden, NY. They take care of their own. There were so many people there all day long, in and out; it was unbelievable. Almost everyone we know is a musician, and Jason's stepfather, Bob Fleming, has been in a band for 30 plus years. They played, and Andy and I played with our band, and Jason's band played. He had a ball. It was so comforting to know that we had so many people who were praying for him every day. He was so loved by everyone!

It was around this time that he started seeing Joann Usyk. She was a few years younger than him but seemed very mature in some senses. They became a couple, and she was constantly there for him. I asked her for some stories, and it was very hard for her. They had broken up a couple years before but were always "on again, off again." I remember they would go through periods where they would be so mad at each other they couldn't even talk, yet somehow would be speaking again when things got scary for him. She even offered to marry him when he couldn't work anymore. She had enlisted in the Army back in 2006, and was stationed at Ft. Bragg, I think. She told him if they got married, he could be covered under her insurance, and she could send him the extra money she would get every month, because he wasn't able to work. It was a nice thought.

Because they were so close shortly after he started his treatment through the first few years, she probably was the one he confided in most, and was most "real" with about the feelings and fear he felt. I asked her to send me something for this book, and she did.

JoAnn writes:
Ok, I am going to do my best. I'm sorry it has taken me so long to do this for you. I am still finding this very hard to deal with even after all this time... this is probably going to be in very random order but I will try to organize it.

I met Jay at a Battle of the Bands - he was watching with Gary (Johnson) and I was singing. A few months later I found out he had gotten diagnosed. We chatted online for months then I went and visited him at Rome Hospital for some random reason, the rest was history. I started visiting him on a regular basis - we decided to form a band. I used the excuse one night that I needed to come bring him my work schedule so we could start booking shows, but instead I walked in with a movie. Visits to Rochester followed and then we were officially dating.

Our first Halloween together, I painted his head, face and neck blue and he went as a blue man from the Blue Man Group - he pulled it off great. We had just started officially dating that month and that was the night I learned how stubborn he was. Gary went out with us and as far as he was concerned (and everyone else) Jay should not be drinking. He was playing pool and every time he ordered a drink, Gary or I would chug it real quick so when Jay turned around it was gone and he couldn't drink it. That backfired on me immensely because I got very drunk (lol). But he insisted and kept ordering more because he refused to make his sickness rule his life, he was

28

going to do what he wanted and nothing was going to dictate how he lived.

He taught me how to set up and break down his set, trying to fix it when I turned around so I wouldn't feel bad about doing it completely wrong.

Jay loved doing things for his brothers, he played the loud dad on the side lines a few times at baseball games. We even got thrown out of a game because he got a little loud with the boys' coach. As much as they would bicker at home, if anyone tried messing with them he was there to take care of it.

One Valentine's day he bought me tickets to see the musical Mama Mia still a few months away, and then he ended up having his surgery a short time after and was still recovering when it came to the day of the show. He had told me that he wouldn't be able to go with me after all, and to just go with my mom. He could barely walk, let alone climb stairs. But sure enough when I walked out of my room to leave the house the night of the show, there he was, sitting on my couch all dressed up with flowers and his pillow. He was bound and determined to follow through and take me on our date like he had promised. We had to walk up flights of stairs to get to our seats and he had to sit on his pillow. I knew he was in so much pain and felt absolutely horrible but he wouldn't take no for an answer. Once again, he was not going to let his sickness mess with his life. He struggled to get through the show but he did and I could tell it was a triumph for him.

Strong Hospital holds many memories. It was saddening and uplifting at the same time to see him interact with the other patients and doctors and nurses- like you would see a college student do with their fellow students and teachers on campus. That was another part of his family. I used to get so sad because it killed me to know he had a relationship with those people due to the Cancer. But then I would realize how great it was that he was dealing with it on a positive level. He wasn't walking around miserable and angry, ignoring people like some people in his position would do, rather embracing it and welcoming people into his life, trying to stay open and positive.

Of course there were down days. There were days we would walk to the chapel and sit and pray for hours, and once he was in the safety of his hospital room he would cry in my arms for the whole night. He was scared. But you better believe the minute any nurse stepped through the door for vitals he pulled himself together instantly. He didn't want people to see him weak, and it was almost like he felt he had to stay strong for everyone around him. I would sit beside him or lay with him in his bed and read to him till he fell asleep. There would be many times that he would wake up and I would be watching TV or doing homework and he would ask me to read him to sleep. It really calmed him. There was a woman who used to go from patient to patient on some days and play her harp. Jay loved that.

I remember after his surgery he was bound

and determined to get up on his feet and walk. He was in a lot of pain, but he wanted to get out of there and back on his feet quickly. He would push himself so much. We would walk to the closet door one day, the next door the next, around the corner the next and before you knew it he was going back to his regular wing to chat with his nurses.

We spent a New Years in the hospital. We brought out hats and noise makers and sparkling juice. At first he wanted to kill me saying it was lame, but once we popped the top you could tell he was enjoying himself.

We used to joke about his cancer being a lie. It may sound messed up and crude but that's how Jay was. He tried to lighten things up when possible. I used to tell him he could stop faking it now because I think he finally had enough time off and he would tell me that if he did that he would have no excuse for his "Chemo farts". Always the funny guy.

I still keep in touch with JoAnn and see her whenever she comes home. I will always be glad that she was there for Jason during those first few years of his illness, and she helped him more than I think anyone knows.

*****

Another relationship Jason developed around the same time as JoAnn was with my cousin, Beverly's son, Brendon Barclay. The year before Jason was diagnosed, Brendon was diagnosed with testicular cancer. My cousin is an RN, and because of her educating her kids on being

31

aware of changes in their bodies, Brendon was able to be diagnosed and treated very early. After enduring intense chemotherapy and treatment, he was declared cancer free, and has celebrated his 5 year survivor landmark.

A few months after Jason was diagnosed, I had been in touch with Beverly trying to get an insider's perspective on the hospital visits, and what to watch for to make sure things were proceeding as they should. I gave Jason Brendon's phone number, and they started to get to know each other because of the common bond. Brendon sent me this story of one of their first meetings.

Growing up, the only time Jason and I saw each other was at family reunions or when we came up to visit every so often. It wasn't until I heard that he was sick (about 6 months after I was diagnosed) that we truly got to know each other. Our weaknesses quickly became our "common ground" and strength for our relationship from that time forward. I remember talking to him on the phone a few times and thinking things would be weird or uncomfortable when we saw each other face to face. That wasn't the case; we became quick friends and closer cousins because of the way we looked at what we had to go through. I remember getting better, then him starting to improve and hopes were high. Of course, he had a rocky road to travel and tolerated it better than anyone I can think of. Because of the way I think about things, and my martial arts training and eastern philosophy I can say that his passion for life and the drums, made him a true warrior and artist.

My fondest memory of us is when I came up from college a few weeks before Halloween one

*year and we got dinner, and hung out with his
then band members from "1224". We hung out at
the house, went to a bar, came back to the house
and then decided to go and get some pumpkins.
We piled into a couple of our trucks (Gary's, and
mine) and headed to Wal-Mart. We picked up
several pumpkins and headed home to carve them.
I remember splitting my pumpkin and asking
Jason if he had anything around that I could
"McGuyver" the pumpkin up with. He headed
upstairs and came back with a busted guitar
string. I thought for a few minutes, my pumpkin in
2 halves, while they all continued to decorate.
Jason offered an idea to tie the string around the
pumpkin, but it kept slipping, so I thought about
poking 2 small holes on either side of the
pumpkin, and stuck the string through them and
tied it inside the pumpkin and it looked like a
Frankenstein pumpkin. We had some good laughs
over it before we turned on the TV and hung out
until we fell asleep.*

*I hope this helps. And I hope you know and
understand how much going through something
so devastating with a friend like Jason, helped me
to get through my own sickness.*

*****

I had no idea at the time what was going to happen,
but I lost my job in December. The new district manager
and I didn't hit it off well at all. But, again, in hindsight, I
think it was time for me to concentrate completely on
Jason, and being there for him. I was so stressed; I am not
sure how long I could have kept up working full time, and

taking care of him, and worrying about him and his care, especially with the gravity of his situation, and the doctors not quite knowing what to do with him, or how to save him.

There's a lot to be said for "fate". My sister, Cheri, had been married to her husband, Dave, for over 20 years. They both have a big family, lots of siblings, cousins, aunts, uncles. In November, 2003, they went to a wedding for someone in Dave's extended family. They were sitting at a table with his parents, one of his aunts, and another man who Cheri didn't know. She asked her father-in-law who the man was, and he said, "That's my nephew, Father Peter! You don't know Father Peter?" She said she had never met him but she had heard about him. He was a healing priest. He traveled around the world doing healing masses. He could tell story after story of how he had witnessed miracles and healing of all kinds. Cheri had never met him because he had been traveling for the previous 25 years or so, but he had recently moved to Ilion, NY, which was only about half an hour from us. She talked to Father Peter, and told him about Jason. She asked him to let us know when he would be doing a mass, so we could come. He said he would let them know.

Shortly after, Dave's mother jokingly called across the table to Father Peter. "Peter, I am not mailing you your Christmas cookies this year. If you want them, you have to come and get them so we can visit with you a little."

He agreed to pick them up at their house which was around the corner from our house. Dave's father talked to Father Peter, and asked him if he would come to their house the next Sunday and they would call Jason and me over, and he could pray with him.

Now, we are not exactly religious by any means. I

believe in God. I used to go to church when I was little, but rarely in my adult life. Jason was baptized, and that was about the extent of it. However, when faced with your mortality or your child's, one can suddenly feel very compelled to find Jesus, and at least introduce yourself.

When Peter came over to the Guggi's (Cheri and Dave's parents), they called us and invited us over for coffee. We walked down to their house, and spent about an hour just sitting at the table, eating cookies, and talking about any and everything. Then, he told us about some of the miracles he had been a part of over the years. He was likable, and approachable, and I think Jason felt more comfortable than either of us thought he would. When we were finished talking, Father Peter asked if we wanted to go into the living room and pray with him. We went in, and he prayed with all of us at first. Then, he came over to Jason and laid his hands on him, and prayed for his healing and continued health. It was very powerful and emotional. Jason said afterwards when we got home that he actually felt a warmth come over him. They say that is the warmth of the Holy Spirit, and many people have felt that in the presence of healers.

That was at the beginning of December. Jay had continued to do the chemo treatments in November and December, but Dr. Khorana was still worried about him getting too much chemo, and the tumor not responding as well as he had expected.

In January, 2004, he had another CT Scan, to see if any more progress had been made. When we went in for the results of the scan, he was ecstatic! He said the tumor had shrunk more in the last three months than it had through the whole time before that. It was a miracle! The tumor was small enough now so they could perform the surgery!

We told Dr. Khorana about Father Peter, and the healing session we had with him. He said he thought that maybe the treatments had something to do with it, too! Ooops.

So, the surgery was scheduled for February. It would be a long surgery, but Dr. Orloff was sure he would be successful in doing a liver resection, and getting the whole tumor. I waited in the lobby with my mother, my sister, Joann, Jason's sister Erin, and even my cousin Patrick's wife, Marybeth, stopped by to see how we were holding up. It was about ten hours before they were done. We were still in the lobby, and Cheri noticed a doctor in scrubs across the lobby.
She said, "Oh, look - there's a doctor with good news for somebody!"

I looked and said, "That's our doctor!"

He came over and told us that the operation was successful! He said, "I'm not supposed to say that we got it all - but I know we got it all! I felt all around, and I'm sure we got it!" He said it was unlike anything he had ever seen. The tumor just "peeled" off in layers and came right out in his hands. I was so excited and relieved, I hugged him!

They had to remove several of the lymph nodes and rebuild a bile duct during the surgery. That's why it took so long. But, Jason did really well, and they expected him to recover and be on the road to "remission." He would have to have two more rounds of the chemo just in case there were some straggling cells still in his system, but they were not worried. What a relief!

He was in pretty rough shape, though, for a while after the surgery. They called the scar the "Mercedes" scar, because it was in the shape of the Mercedes logo. He called himself "Scar Belly" and wore it like a badge.

According to Jason's notes, he was in "remission", although I don't remember the doctors actually saying those words. In June 2004, they decided he had recovered enough from the surgery to do the two more rounds of chemo. After that, he would be cancer free. He still did CT scans every three months to keep everything in check.

He started to feel normal again. He was going to go back to school in January. He got a job and started back up with his band playing drums. It was like he just took a year and a half off, and was given a new lease on life. We both tried to just put it behind us, and get back to some sort of "post cancer" normalcy.

Jason had a scan done in October and it was clear. He moved to Syracuse with JoAnn, and enrolled in school for the January semester. I wasn't back to work yet, so I was helping out my brother and sister-in-law babysitting for them. Life was getting back to normal.

*****

Until January, 2005. Jason went for his CT Scan, and went back for the results on a Friday. I didn't go with him, because it had become pretty routine, and I was babysitting the girls. I told Jason to call me on his way home. Dr. Khorana called me himself. Honestly, my first thought was, "Gees, what a great guy, he is calling me to give me an update himself!" Unfortunately, it wasn't a courtesy call.

37

"I'm sorry," he said. "The scan showed a small spot in the tissue near where the lymph nodes were removed during the surgery." I burst into tears.

"NO!" I screamed into the phone. I couldn't believe it. We were just getting back to normal. How can this be happening! All I could think of was Jason driving back from Rochester, alone, with this news. I can't believe I didn't go with him, I thought.

I called my parents. They had just left for Florida that morning to see my sister and her family. I had to tell my mother. She had the same reaction I did, but I don't think she could speak at first. She asked if they should turn around and come home, but there didn't seem to be any point in that. I told her when we knew what we had to do, I would call them and let them know. They may as well get away and try to relax a little, if possible.

In February, 2005, Jason resumed the PIAF chemotherapy again. He had three more cycles - total of 13 now. Even though they were worried about him having too much of the chemo, they considered his age to be an advantage, and were semi-comfortable pushing the limits a little. But, he didn't respond to the treatments. The cancer was spreading.

I believe he had three different spots they were dealing with at that point. He had one in the tissue around the liver resection site, one behind his esophagus, and one near his heart. None of them seemed to be responding to the chemo anymore. We needed a new plan.

At that time, he was referred to Dr. Katz at Strong for radiation therapy. He was to do radiation treatments on the masses on a very precise radiation machine called the Novalis Focused Beam. It was a relatively new machine which targeted the specific cancerous cells but spared the healthy tissue surrounding them. I think it was somewhat successful, but not quite what they had hoped for.

They had another chemo they were going to try on Jason. It had to be administered through an IV as an inpatient, but they said we could see an oncologist closer to home to cut down on our travel cost and time. We were referred to a Dr. Thomas Ryan at St. Elizabeth hospital in Utica. The drug was Gemzar - a very strong chemotherapy drug. He would get the infusion and wait two weeks to get his blood levels back up.

The first treatment was tough on him, but he was ok to have the next infusion the following cycle. After the second treatment, Jay went in for his blood work, and his WBC was much lower than they needed it to be. They were supposed to be under the direction of Dr. Khorana at Strong. Dr. Ryan said he had called Dr. Khorana and relayed the information, and according to him, Dr. Khorana said he could still do the full dose of chemo.

Shortly after getting the infusion, Jason suddenly developed a very high temp (104°), and became very sick. It seemed they had overdosed him on the Gemzar. I brought him to the emergency room at St. Elizabeth's Hospital, but we found out that he was not supposed to get that full dose of chemo, and we lost confidence in Dr. Ryan. We had him transferred to Rome Hospital, where Dr. Kirk could monitor him, and hopefully get him back to a safe state. After two or three days in ICU, they transferred him to Strong by ambulance, and they were finally able to get his temperature and vitals back under control. The whole ordeal took about two weeks to get him back to normal.

I found an update he had sent to his family and friends after he was back home and back on track.

Subject: The Update
10/25/05

> ALIVE AND WELL!! Ha-ha. Seriously though, I'm home now, after my two week
stint in the 3 hospitals and all that good stuff. I'm feeling great, I just
had to get through a little bump in the road but I'm back home and at 100% so
everyone QUIT WORRYING!! =) I'm kidding - I really do appreciate all the support
and calls and everything. From what I understood granddad sent out about 300
updates so I think everyone was pretty well informed as to what was going on
which makes things a little easier for me, so thank you Granddad. Aside from
that though, the tumors both actually shrank about 2.5 centimeters from the
last scans, so the chemo overdose wasn't a complete set back in that respect.
So things are looking good. As for future treatments, they're going to be
starting me on a one a day pill at home.   This type of chemotherapy has been
tested and had the best results on lung cancers so far, but Dr. Khorana has used it on his liver
cancer patients with some success. I've yet to find out if it affects the liver itself, or the TYPE of cells
that are considered liver cancer. Either way my

oncologist (who wears his heart on his sleeve,
which can be good and bad) is very optimistic
about this new chemo and has seen very good
results, especially like I mentioned, with liver
cancers. So this should help me to get my life back
in order a little bit with less doctor
visits and such. I think that's about it for now, if I
hear anything new
I'll be sure to email everyone and let them know
what's going on, but for now things
are finally calmed down again and back to
normal. Thanks again everyone for
the prayers and support. Love you guys!!

> Love Jay

> PS ~ I wasn't kidding about a family
reunion....next year maybe? =)

I wish I had had the foresight to save all of the "Jason Update" emails we sent from the beginning of the treatment. I would send some, or he would send them, but they were always like a window into our inner thoughts, whether wide open, or just behind the shade. But, he always put the "Jason Spin" on them to make sure that everyone knew he was "doing great and not to worry."

As Jason said, while the chemo overdose was definitely a scary and life threatening situation, it may have shrunk some of his tumors. Dr. Khorana switched him to a daily pill called Tarceva to try to keep the tumors in check, which it seemed to do for over a year. He would go for the CT Scans every three months, and although the "spots" weren't going away, they were not growing either, so that was considered "successful."

41

In 2006, we all went down to Florida on vacation for one of the boy's breaks - I can't remember if it was in February or April. We went to Cheri and Dave's for the first few days, and to Disney for the last four days. We really had a great time, and Jason was feeling very good the whole week. My niece, Julie, sent me a story about that week. I decided not to edit it, and let it flow the way she sent it.

So I guess it had to be 2006, the month is undetermined... no one in the Guggi household can figure it out... Jay and the family came down on vacation... yes if you can imagine it, Jay and his whole family and the Guggi's under one roof! My story is about taking Jay to this 3 story club, that had $1 drinks... top shelf, you call it, anything in the world... for $1.

So we had been talking about this place called "Brick Town 54" for a couple days now. I told Jay it was this massive dance club, 5 bucks to get in and $1 anything in the world.

He was like, "Wait a minute? $1 anything? Like Jack and coke? Crown? Beer? Shots?!" I was like, " Yes!! Anything!" So, Monday night came around, and we had decided to go out. It was sure enough, time for Brick Town! I, of course, had a few beautiful blonde friends meeting us out there, whom Jay was naturally inclined to fall in love with... ha-ha...

It's about 10pm now, and Jay and I are dressed to impress and ready to go.

The place was, luckily, only 5 minutes from my house. We get there, wait in the incredibly long line, pay our 5 bucks and get in. We turned the corner, and all of a sudden, it's 3 levels of just pure chaos. Beer girls with tubs as soon as you *walk in, a bar in every corner of the place and platforms for dancing on; Jay just looks at me and says, "Juj, holy sh*t!" So as we dance the night away, (with my beautiful blonde friends…) and drink after drink…. and drink after drink.. and I, of course, had to be responsible because I was driving. But Jay kept going, drink after drink (if my mind serves me right I believe it was a whole lotta Jack & coke).*

(I will add also that I said "Jay, watch out, just because the drinks are a dollar doesn't mean you need to drink this place dry" pssst!- he didn't listen to me)

So the story gets more interesting as we leave. Jay is hammered and just elated at the great night we had. We search the parking lot for my car and finally find it. Now, I already told you that I only live 5 minutes away from this place, however it took us much longer to get home. We get 2 blocks down from the club, and Jay is like " Juj I'm gonna puke." I'm like, " Awww, Jay, come on now!" So I pulled over and literally had to run to his door so he wouldn't puke in my car…. He does his deed and we are on our way again. Then we finally make it to the house.

I parked the car and went to Jay's door because he "fell asleep". I shake him to get him up, however he thought at this point, the front lawn was a better bed than the couch. So at this point he's literally laying on the front lawn, all curled up ready for bed. I'm like, "Oh hell no Jay!" As I shake him and shake him to get him up, he ends up puking again. We make it to the front door. I drag him through the living room to the back porch. I figured that that would be the safest place in case he had a few more episodes. I

put him on the couch, grabbed the garbage can,
some water and a blanket, and tucked him in.

His look in the morning was like, "$1 drinks!
Uggghhh!"

We did have a ball that whole week. Jason left
early because he had to play with the band on Saturday
night, but I will always be thankful that we took that trip
when we did. We have great memories to keep forever.

One particular memory is the day we went to Epcot.
We walked in early in the morning, and posing for photos
in front of the Epcot ball was an entire team or two of a
girl's high school soccer team. Jason just looked and
stopped in his tracks, grinning from ear to ear. Being the
mom, and never missing an opportunity to mortify my
children, I went up to the group and asked them if they
would stay for a quick photo with Jason in the middle of
them. At first he turned beet red but, being Jay, almost
immediately jumped right in and took the picture!
Priceless.

*****

Jay moved in with his friend and band mate, Nick
Visalli, sometime in 2006, I think. He was having such a
hard time without having a car, and we were literally at
each other's throats most of the time. He tried to have as
normal a life as he could, and we both tried to move
forward. He started working, and was very happy to be
performing with "Coersion" (pre The Blueprint), and he
would find jobs that he could manage to get to easily.

He became fast friends with Nick, and they were as
close as brothers. Nick had so many memories he wanted

to write about, he found it hard to limit it to this email.

Nick Visalli writes:

> *There are more stories than I could ever dream of writing about my dear friend Jay, but I will try to get as many of them down...*

> *I guess it all started on that summer day out in Sylvan Beach when our band Coersion was playing at Phol's beach house. Our current drummer was my cousin Kenny, who had decided to leave the band to pursue his medical career. This band, The Morning After, opened up for us and played this acoustic set and had this kid playing a bongo drum. Come to find out, this was just their sound guy, Jay. Well, this Jay kid started talking to our manager (Smooth) about us and found out we were looking for a drummer. After our set Jay approached us all and told us how much he liked us and how interested he was in playing with us. We exchanged screen names and what not, but I figured nothing much would come from it. We already had someone picked out that we were pretty sure would be our next drummer anyway.*

> *During that week Jay IMed me and would not stop talking about how much he wanted to join our band. After talking to him I was starting to think we should give him a chance. It was the best thing that ever happened to our band and the beginning of the best two and a half years of my life.*
> *I remember the first time Jay showed up at my house with an electronic drum set to practice*

our songs and he knew everything perfectly. After about two weeks Jay had already found us a spot to practice. And that's pretty much how everything in the band went for the next two and a half years. He loved this band with all his heart and gave his life to it.

After about 2 months of being in the band, Jay broke up with his girlfriend at the time and needed a place to stay for "2 weeks". Well, those two weeks turned into about 2 years, and it was by far the most fun I have had in my life. Jay was just always down to party and have a good time. He did get frustrated at times with being sick especially when it came back, but never once to me did he say, "Why me?", or complain about it. Only when I asked about what was going on and told him to tell me everything would he talk to me about it.

One of my memories that I loved was every night when we went out, whether we were together or separate we would come home and talk for a good half hour to an hour about our night, and what was going on in our lives. Of course, it would usually be me rambling on, and Jay listening to me and giving me advice. Then the rest would be about the band.

When it came to the band I can say honestly he was the heart and soul of Coersion/the Blueprint. We all loved it, we all love playing and writing music, but there is so much more to being in a band than just playing. There's so much that goes on behind the scenes, and Jay took care of all that. You could not have a conversation with Jay without the band coming up. My best memories of my life are with the band. Being on the road with Jay was always a riot. I'll never forgot the time we got pulled over in Ohio, and the cop came up to the car and asked what we were doing and Jay told him we were in a band just got done playing a show. So the cop asked, sort of joking, if we had dead bodies in the van. So of course, Jay says to the cop in the most serious manner, "well, we are from New York, so you never know.".

It wasn't just on the road that we would have fun. We pretty much played every weekend and after parties were some of the best times. There was the time Jay came out in Shelby's bikini and stayed in it all night, which was probably one of the funniest things I have ever seen.

In general Jay was always the one who wanted to keep the party going and always wanted everyone to be together. It was Jay who had the idea of Festivus every year at Christmas time so that all of his friends from Camden and Utica could have a place to get together and have a great time. It was Jay who, whenever we played in NYC, made sure to get every single person we possibly could together to come down with us and have a great time. There was nothing that Jay loved more than having all of his friends get together to just hang out and have a good time.

There are so many more things I could write about in the three years I knew Jay. It seems like a short time, but so much went on during that time. Jay taught me so much on how to live my life, to live everyday to the fullest and like it's your last. He always told me that he wanted to go to bed every night knowing that he couldn't have possibly done anymore. He did more and I think had more of an effect on people in his 25 years than most people will in a lifetime.

Even in his last week he always looked out for everyone else, didn't want anyone else to worry about him, told everyone he was doing ok. That brings me to my last story of Jay and one that pretty much sums up what Jay is all about and what he meant to me. On the day that Jay passed, (I believe it was about 1 or 1:30 which was pretty close to when he passed....)Jay sent me a text telling me that I was the best friend a person could ever have, and that he loved me, and was grateful for everything I had done for him. Jay knew how I am, and knew that hearing that would help me in the rough times I would have going forward without him. Even in his moments of death, Jay was thinking of other people, thanking other people for help.

Jay wasn't just a drummer to me, or just a friend. After living with him for two years, he was my third brother, and also another son to my mom and dad. It was a short time, but I am so grateful to have had Jay in my life. There is not a day that goes by that I don't think of Jay, or want him back so badly. But of course even now that he is gone, he still helps me, still sends signs to all of us that he is watching over us. The last two times we have been setting up for a show "Let it be" by the Beatles has come on the radio, and it always comes on when something is going wrong while we are setting up. Just Jay telling us not to stress out and everything will be fine. There was also the time that I was having an awful time dealing with it and I told Jay to just send me a sign that he is there. I was at a bar, and about two minutes later, a kid walked in the bar that looked almost identical to Jay, and all of us just looked at each other because we all were thinking the same thing. The kid sat next to us and ordered a Jack and coke, which was Jay's drink of choice.

Jay cared about everyone else almost more than he did himself, and always tried to help other people. I think that it's amazing that not only do we have stories of Jay from his life, but we can also tell stories about him from after he passed. Jay is still here with us all the time, making sure we do what he always wanted us to.......to love our lives.

Jason became close with the other band members as well. Sam was their lead singer, and songwriter, and apparently, they may have gotten off to a rough start, but formed a close relationship quickly. If I had known the thing that secured their "bond" ahead of time, I would have kicked both of their asses!

Sam Famolaro
vocals, rhythm guitar with "the Blueprint"

I met Jay Wilhelm for the first time at the infamous basement in Nick Visalli's house. I had just previously been informed that Jay was the new drummer. I remember being angry that Nick had gone out and found someone who I had never met, without asking for my help, but Jay seemed like the right choice almost from the second I met him. He was smart and charismatic and he had a deep, burning desire to make this band something really special. Jay and I did not always see eye-to-eye in our friendship, as a matter-of-fact, we very rarely agreed on anything. But as time went on, what started out as a cold, business like-respect turned into a kind of admiration for each other's stubbornness, and soon enough, he was one of my best friends on the planet.

It's probably not a great thing to admit, but the thing that brought Jay and I closer together was smoking cigarettes. I feel bad saying that, but knowing Jay, I don't think he would have minded. We were the only smokers in the band. Nick and Kevin actually used to rag on us all the time for it, so we would always sneak out of the basement and go for these long epic walks up and down James Street. During which time, we would admire the ghetto and smoke Parliament Lights or Camel Wides (depended on who was bumming cigarettes from who) and solve all of the worlds problems. We'd talk about the Yankees and we'd make fun of Steve's stupid Red Sox tattoo or we'd have heated debates about Yes and Jimmy Eat World. We talked about girl problems, money problems, and work problems... as you can see, we had our share of problems. I respected Jay's opinion and he respected mine, and because of it, I trusted him more that anyone I knew. If I could convince Jay, I could convince anyone and if I had Jay's approval, I knew I didn't need anyone else's.

I think we were in Sandusky, Ohio staying at a little hotel on some unknown strip-mall suburbia. It was one of tour numerous Midwestern "VanZilla" Tours (VanZilla was the name of our

*van by the way. It was my idea and Jay approved.
Further proof that as long as I had Jay's approval,
I didn't need anyone else's). Jay loved touring more
than anything else. When we were on the road he
was like a different person. His eyes were a little bit
wider and his voice was more alive. We felt like we
were justified on the road. It was like we had
escaped all the people back home who hated the
band or said we were wasting our time. It was us
against the world, Five Against One. We weren't
family, but when we were on the road together you
couldn't tell the difference. Our friend's Melissa
and Sarah had come out to see us, and so had our
friend Mandy and few of her friends as well. I was
having a fight with my girlfriend at the time, so
while everyone else was off having our own little
hotel party, I was outside on the roof of the van on
my phone arguing. Jay came outside, and climbed
up next to me. He sat with me for a few minutes
and Jay started telling me how I should look
around and remember where we were; how lucky
we were to be on the road, living out the things we
had talked about for so long. And just as it seemed
like he was about to go off on one of his patented
speeches, he suddenly remembered that all of our
beer was inside and we unfortunately were outside.*

*"You stay here, I'm getting some beers,
and I'm coming right back" was pretty close to
what he said as he leapt off the van and ran inside.*

*Literally the second the door closed behind
him, a police car wheels into the parking lot, pulls
me off the van (apparently, I looked like a cat
burglar or something) and tells me to put my
hands on the car and keep them there. I see Jay*

51

walk out of our room, with 6 bottles of beer in his hand, turn to look at me, and I watch his jaw hit the ground. He went from excited (about the prospect of beer on the roof of the van) to petrified (about presumably having to bail me out of jail) in one second flat. But, undaunted, Jay threw the bottles into the bushes like a ninja, and was successful at "politely" convincing the officers that I was indeed allowed to be on OUR van. Just a quick example of Jay keeping me out of trouble.

Jay-There is a spot in my heart that you filled while you were alive that no one can ever or will ever be able to fill. I had never met anyone like you before and I don't think I'll ever meet anyone like you again. You were a special person and I miss you every single day. I know you are looking out for me, and occasionally having a laugh at my expense, from wherever you are right now. You were not just the drummer, or just my friend. You were like a brother to me, like the brother I never had. I know that I'll see you again one day, and until then you'll have to keep everyone entertained by yourself.

I know you're up to it.
five against one.

*****

I went back to work, and I remember figuring out that the only way to handle the situation was to block it out when ever I had to think about anything else. So, I created somewhat of a "room" in my mind, and I would put the situation in the room, and lock the door during the day. By doing that, it enabled me to function somewhat normally, without losing it during the day. I tried to only think about Jason's situation when I had to, when we went to Rochester for check ups, or if he was having a problem. And most of the time it worked. I think he must have done the same, although, with him being out of the house, I had less information than I had the previous three years.

I can't remember exactly when it was, but I think it was sometime in 2007, Jason went to a Kid Rock concert with his friend, Shelby Armstrong, and her family. Her mom, Shereen, had cancer, and she and Jason had become friends because of their common concerns. I asked Shelby to send me a story about the Kid Rock concert, and anything else she wanted.

> *I can remember this one time we all went to watch the boys play a show in Syracuse. Like always it was an amazing show. After that we all drove back to Steve's house to hang out and what not. A few of us decided that we were going to go swimming, so we were all outside hanging out on the deck of the pool having a good time and next thing you know here comes Jay walking out in my bathing suit that I had left at Steve's. He had even stuffed it to make it look like he was a girl. Everyone just looked at him, laughing hysterically. Jay stood there in the bathing suit with a smirk and said to all of us "What guys? I thought we were going swimming..." It was one of the funniest things I've seen because we weren't expecting it at all. There are actually pictures of it.*

> *Another thing I can remember is one night we were all hanging out at Sam's house just watching __The Godfather,__ I believe, and I had been*

in a bad mood because of things that were going on in my family with my mom. Jay could always tell when someone was upset, and he always would try and do whatever he could to make you feel better. He took me out on the porch and we talked forever. I was having a hard time dealing with my mom's cancer and everything that was going on, and I didn't know how to cope with it or talk to my mom about it. Jay sat there and told me from his perspective what he would want if he was in my mom's spot and how its ok to talk about it even if it isn't all good. Then he told me the story about when he got diagnosed and just sat with his mother for hours until the sun came up, and he saw birds on the ground, and how at that moment, he knew everything was going to be ok. I didn't know why at the time. but for some reason that story made me feel so much better, and made me realize that things would be ok. That I could get through what I was dealing with, and that he would be there to help if I ever needed someone to talk to.

My cousin dates Jimmy Bones who is the keyboardist for Kid Rock. My mom got tickets and passes for us all to go to a concert at Casino Niagara in Buffalo. My mom had been talking to Jimmy about how amazing Jay was at playing drums, and had been sending them videos and CD's of The Blueprint playing. Jimmy and the drummer, Stephanie, really enjoyed their music and Jimmy wanted to meet Jay. So my mom, two sisters, jay and I all went to the show. I remember listing to The Blueprint the whole way up there. The hotel was amazing. Jay and my mom went down to the bar to have a drink before the show.

While they were down there they met a man who asked them if they were here for the show and they said yes. Then he asked them if they were ready to "Partay!", and Jay said yes- and my mom told the man that she brought her ear plugs!

We had amazing seats, very close to the stage. Jay and my sister went up closer to the stage where people were jumping around singing and dancing, and then returned when security made everyone go back and sit down. I'm never going to forget Jay and my mom's face when Rev Run came on the stage to perform, they both looked at each other in shock. The man that had talked to them earlier to see if they were ready to party was Rev Run! The performance that Kid Rock and all his guests put on was amazing! I don't think I've ever seen a show as good.

After the show we went back up to our hotel room to wait for Jimmy to call us to go to his room. When we were in Jimmy's room, Stephanie (the drummer), came to meet Jay. They didn't have a lot of time because Kid Rock had left right after the show and they had to hurry and get ready to go get on the bus and leave. They ended up sitting upstairs for about a half an hour to 45 minutes talking to Jay about his drumming and music. Jimmy ended up giving Jay one of his harmonicas that he had used to record a song for Tim McGraw, and that he had used in the show that night. In return, Jay gave them some more CD's of his, and even gave them each a t-shirt. Stephanie was very thankful about that because she said now she had something to listen to on the bus. The band wasn't staying at the hotel that night but the Casino had given them the rooms for the night so Jimmy ended up giving his hotel room to Jay for the night. I'm never going to forget how happy Jay looked with how that night turned out.

Jason did have a ball that night, although he felt a little strange being the only man with all those women! He was a little disappointed that he didn't get to meet Kid Rock, but the reception and time he spent with Jimmy and Stephanie more than made up for it. He talked about it for a long time after.

I, on the other hand, was very disappointed that he didn't get to meet Kid Rock, although I didn't say that to Jay. I know that people have limited time when they are in that position, but I think it would have meant the world to Jay if he just stuck his head in the room and shook his hand. But, then, I am his mother! So, if anyone reading this has access to Kid Rock, perhaps you could let him know that it wasn't Jason who missed out on the opportunity to meet him. But rather, his loss in not taking a moment to shake the hand of a man hundreds admired and loved for his great character, unconditional love, and unending ability to make everyone who met him feel blessed for the chance. Of course, you could also tell him that a nice donation to Jason's fund would more than make up for his unwittingly missed opportunity!

*****

He continued on the Tarceva for a year, but then it must have stopped working because Dr. Khorana changed it to another daily pill. There were three or four of them throughout the end of 2006 to 2007, but none of them were successful at all.

Then, in October of 2007, his CT scan showed that the cancer had metastasized to his lungs. They estimated he had around fifty "nodules" on his lungs. FIFTY. They immediately set up a radiation session with Dr. Katz. He wanted to do 16 rounds of radiation on the Novalis machine - three weeks, Monday through Friday.

I stayed in Rochester with him at the Hope Lodge. My company, had an office in Greece, NY, that was not far from the Hope Lodge and the hospital. I was able to switch offices with the manager of that office for three weeks while Jason went through his treatment.

The first night, he was sick, scared, and just completely down. He didn't get like that often, but I couldn't imagine what it must be like knowing you have this monstrosity growing inside you, out of control, and all you can do is keep throwing stuff at it trying to slow it down. It was hard for me to find the strength to help him keep fighting. I called my mother and had her come to Rochester the next day to stay with us. I needed her, but I also knew that Jason would want to be strong for HER. He wouldn't want her to get upset, so he would force himself to stay as positive as possible. I think it worked, but possibly more for me than for him at the time.

It was also in October, 2007, that Jason's friend Erica Schultz' mom was stricken at home with a brain aneurysm. Jason was so concerned for Erica and what she was going through, that I think it overshadowed what he was going through. Erica sent me her story. I am so glad that Jay could be there for her to lean on, even if she was kicking and screaming that she didn't need it. Here is her story.

You know I could always tell he cared, but

57

hearing from you that he actually talked to you about what I was going through and the trouble I had, really shows me even more how much he cared, and how amazing he was. I can tell the story but you will have to bear with me because all if it is embedded in my head like an awful nightmare, so it may turn out to be very long and detailed.

Everything began on the 28th of October. I left my mom and sister home to carve pumpkins while I went to dinner with a friend of mine to Teddy's. As we were about to leave, I got a text from my sister saying mom was going to the hospital. I quickly called my house and my grandmother picked up which I knew wasn't a good sign. She told me the ambulance was there and taking mom to St. Luke's Hospital. I quickly drove myself to the hospital and actually beat the ambulance there. I waited outside and when it finally arrived, I ran to the doors. They opened and I heard my mom let out a loud scream. She was holding her head, crying. I told the EMTs I was her daughter and they allowed me to follow them. They told her I was there and she reached for my hand. I told her I was there and everything was ok.

They brought her into a room, did an initial exam ,and told me it was nothing but a bad migraine. Then a minute later she stopped screaming. I looked into the room, saw her unconscious and screamed for a doctor. I started to panic. They brought me to the waiting room so I could be with my grandma, aunt and cousin. I called my dad and told him something wasn't right and we needed him to come.

About a half hour later, they called me in and told me she had an aneurysm on her brainstem that burst. The only chance she had of living was if they put in an immediate shunt into her head to drain the blood. It was then they told me she did not have a health care proxy and legally, I was it. I told them to do anything that would keep her alive. Thinking the worst, my dad and I called the rest of my family and our priest and had them come up just in case things didn't work out for the best.

One of the EMTs happened to be a neighbor of mine who is in the process of becoming a priest. He stayed all night with us, leading in prayer, hoping for a miracle. About 1 in the morning, they were finally done and said she had made it through the procedure, but we were not out of the woods. The next morning we got a call from a doctor at Strong Memorial (Jason's hospital) saying he was willing to help. I called my grandma and aunt and had them drive up so they would be there when she got there and my dad, sister and I sat in the parking lot and watched the helicopter take off that afternoon. She was brought to ICU and examined there. They told us she was most likely going to be in a coma for a good amount of time. So we booked a hotel room for the week.

The next day, the day before Halloween, she woke up and pulled the breathing tube out of her mouth. I walked in that morning to see her sitting. It was the biggest miracle I could ever ask for. She was so upset that we were there and my little sister was not going trick or treating the next night. She made jokes, and was upset they shaved half her head. She had her first surgery that day which lasted 3 hours. When she came out, she was still awake which astonished all the doctors. They called her their miracle patient.

We ran home that night after eight when visiting hours ended, and packed a bag of her things so she would be comfortable, then drove back up immediately. The next day was Halloween. We had my sister dress up and go up to her and say trick or treat. She was so happy, not wanting anyone to leave. At eight we left again and she called over and over (since she had her cell phone). The meds were kicking in because she was saying a "burping ghost" was keeping her up all night and wanted me to yell at him so she could get her rest. She told me about all the noise he made and when she told me to listen, it was obvious it was all the beeps from the machines she was connected to. It put a smile on my face. She rubbed in my face that all the doctors think she is a miracle, told me she loved me, and fell asleep.

The next morning was the exact same thing, being a little brat, calling herself a miracle and making jokes. Things seemed to be getting better. That Sunday they took her out of ICU, but I think the transition was too much for her. She started getting worse again, complaining of bad headaches. She fell back into a coma on Monday and had a stroke Tuesday. She had another surgery to try to open up the arteries in her brain hoping the clots would stop. When that didn't work they tried one more surgery Friday.

After taking CT scans, they pulled us into a conference room Saturday. She had been unresponsive since Monday. They pulled up the scans on the computer and it showed her entire head was covered in blood. The stroke she suffered was massive and destroyed her entire brain. They said she would live the life of a "vegetable" and would never wake up; she was brain dead. I knew then what I had to do, but called my entire family up so they could at least say goodbye.

On Sunday the 11th of November, my whole family was there. We went in one by one to say our goodbyes. When it was time, we all held hands, the doctors looked at me. I nodded, and they pulled the plug. We all yelled we loved her and said we'll see her soon. At 2:06 she was pronounced dead. As I sat there all I could think of was maybe I made a wrong decision with her operations. It was me who gave consent for everything that happened to her - maybe it was all my fault.

I sat in the hospital waiting room starring out the window in absolute shock that she was actually gone. The only thing I have good to look back on are those few days I had with her and that I got to tell her I loved her. I'll never forget that. I took those for granted thinking she was going to come out of this ok. I now realize how precious that time really was and I wouldn't trade it for the world.

Every month for 6 months on the 11ᵗʰ, Jay would call me. We would fight because I wouldn't cry or talk about how I felt about my mother's death. He told me I was a stubborn brat and to get over myself, to be a little girl for once and cry. I would call him an ass and hang up. Then, I would cry and it was like he knew. He would call me back and say, "Are you ready to talk?", and I would go on and on about the most random stuff, like a little baby.

And when I was done, he would tell me to stop crying so I could keep up my stubborn, "tough girl" image, and that he wouldn't tell anyone I spent 20 minutes crying.

I miss that. I miss him yelling at me, calling me a pain in the ass. Getting into fights because I wouldn't open up and cry to him. I miss him telling me I'm being unreasonable. I miss him telling me to stop being tough and to just be a girl for once. Most of all, I miss him telling me my mom is still here with me, giving me comfort when I needed it most.

He strived to be my comforter, constantly giving me advice in everything. He was the only one out of all my friends who made sure I was ok every single day of every single month. No one really knew how close he and I were. I made him text me all the time when he had to go to Rochester for treatments, and made him tell me everything the doctors said, even if it was news I didn't want to hear. He knew almost everything about me.

When my mom died, I lost a big part of myself; with him gone, its like another part of me just went away. Words can't express how much I miss him and need him to get through these days to come. I miss the kid who would tell me he loved me by saying "less than what?" referring to the less than three symbol to make a heart <3. I call his phone every now and again just to hear his voice on his voicemail. It puts me to sleep while the only drumstick that I have that is not snapped lays on the side of my bed.

Tammy, I want you to know that Jay was amazing to me throughout that entire time. He told me to have faith and to keep my head up. He gave me words of wisdom and comfort when I needed it the most, and when I told him Saturday that I had to pull the plug the next day, he was ready to drive up immediately to be there with me. I told him to stay home and that I would be ok. He'd text me every night I was there to make sure I was ok, and to get updates on her status.

I've never told that full story before and I would like to think that it was the two of them that gave me the strength to do it just now. It's so hard having the last image of my mom as her turning pale and watching her die with her hand in mine. The Tuesday Jay passed away, I texted him earlier in the day and asked how he was doing. He said he couldn't breathe. Then a few hours later, I got the horrible call that he had passed. I took the day I went to the hospital to visit him with Shelby for granted as well and I kick myself every day for it. He was such an amazing friend to me and was my strength for months. He kept me going. You

*raised a phenomenal son, I could never express
my gratitude to him for everything he did for me. I
lost two of the most important people in my life in
just 6 months, and if they can't be here with me
then at least I have the two most amazing
guardian angels by my side and for that I consider
myself lucky.*

Jason was so concerned about Erica at that time that
he chose to stay home for Thanksgiving, instead of going to
Florida with us. The Blueprint was going to play a show
the night before Thanksgiving, and they were going to
surprise her by making it a benefit for her. He thought
about it for probably five minutes, and said he felt it was
something he needed to do. This was the month after he
found out about his cancer basically exploding in his lungs.
Amazing!

At this point, though, Jason was having a hard time
functioning normally. He had stopped working because
between the treatments, the pain he was having, and his
lowered energy levels, it just made it too hard for him. He
was having a tougher and tougher time playing drums with
the band. He would even bring Tommy out to play with
them, because he knew he couldn't do a full show; so he
would play some, and let Tommy play when he got tired.

There were not many times throughout the entire
ordeal that Jason let his situation get the best of him - at
least not in public. He was so strong and proud, and
instead of whining or complaining, chose to try to be a rock
for all of the people who counted on him. I recently found
this blog on his MySpace page that showed a bit more
vulnerability than he liked to reveal to everyone.

Nov 5, 2007 2:30 AM

Eroticisms in the key of disconsolation

For those of you who are wondering what's going on with me...my health, my band, my short fused antics.....it's all right here. I don't do this often, so I'm going with the "go big or go home" theory .

On a serious note...For anyone that saw my bulletin (that I have since retracted) I want to clear up a few things. Upon re-reading the whole thing I think that it came across wrong, and that without being in my shoes, you wouldn't understand. So, let me try again.

First and foremost, I owe an apology to my band mates and friends for being compulsive and losing my head briefly. I posted that bulletin without as much as talking to them, and for that I am sorry.

Now as far as me being sick: For those of you who, again, don't already know (which is probably a lot of people, since I've been pretty low on the whole thing..). I have nearly fifty tumors across my two lungs. I have another large tumor behind my esophagus, pushing on my airway, challenging my breathing even more. I have another medium sized tumor near my heart as well, which is another prominent threat. I was in Rochester for a month doing radiation treatment. It's been kicking my ass. I can't breathe. I feel seconds from being escorted to the hospital after every show with the band. I'm fighting an addiction to Oxycodone, which is always a possibility when you're taking heavy acting pain medication. I'm actually not even supposed to be playing but it's the only thing that keeps me grounded at all. I don't sleep much at night, since its time I get to myself, yet ironically, I sleep all day because with no one around, and me not being at work, I get lonely.

I'm moving back in with my mother at the end of the week. I don't wanna put the band in jeopardy, but with everything going on, I feel, as I explained to my band earlier, unstable at best. I don't cry over spilled milk; I want to murder over spilled milk. I'm always at my wits end and it's not a healthy way to live. I figure maybe going home, having that comfort level up, having help from my family...will get me back on track.

So as far as me quitting the band...it's the last thing I want to let happen, and I'm going to do anything I can to make sure I don't have to. We'll definitely be playing the SHIT outta NY though, I can tell you that. Touring for right now is a little tricky, but we'll figure it out.

I guess all in all, I just wanna thank my close friends who I don't need to name...because I call or txt most of you at 2:00AM....the REAL close ones get the 5:30AM texts lol.

So yeah....Sorry for being so closed up lately and everything, but it's all pretty much spilling out here...this is what I got. Feel free to comment, or write me on it or call me out on any of it...it's all out there.

Just Jay Wilhelm

Of course, his band and his friends
responded with a resounding -NO PROBLEM.

Kevin Sullivan wrote:

*Let me be the first to say that we
understand and are behind you one-hundred and
ten percent, and anything you ever need I'm right
here. I couldn't imagine what it would be like to
have to shoulder the load that you have, and I'm
constantly impressed with how well you deal with
it all. We're gonna make it through all of this
madness and come out even stronger on the other
side. Stay up.*
Posted by Kevin on Nov 5, 2007 11:41 AM

*****

I think it was back in January or February when
Jason started to "put his affairs in order" or, compiling his
"bucket list." I am not even sure if he realized it at first,
and I certainly didn't until much later. He started spending
more time with Tom and Joe, and really talking to them.
He had one of his friends who takes pictures for the band,
Luke Emrich, come over to our house and take pictures of
him, Tom, and Joe, to give to me for Mother's Day, on a
digital photo frame. (Luke brought me a DVD of every
picture he had ever taken of Jason over the years.
Priceless!) Jason wasn't one to get things done ahead of
time - he was just like his mother, and usually did
everything at the last minute. But he had thought about this
for a long time, and got it done by early March. It was
beautiful.

It was also in January when he started talking about

67

having a party for his "5 year Survivor" anniversary. He wanted to have a party - NOT a benefit, not a get-together, but a full blown party to have all of his friends and family get together to celebrate with him. It was so good for him because he was so excited about it, and it gave him something to look forward to.

Believe it or not, we didn't really talk much about his condition, and how he felt about it. We never had the "What if" talk, or even thought aloud about the worst case scenario. If I had to guess, I would say it was probably because neither one of us could stand to have the other one upset about the situation, so we just didn't talk about it. I found a post he sent out on his MySpace page to his friends.

> *Mar 9, 2008 4:02 PM*
> *Since October*
> *Some of you know and some don't and I suppose this is for both. In October I started Radiation therapy along with another type of Chemotherapy to try to combat the 50+ tumors in my lungs, chest and surrounding areas. Since then I've been through another 4 types of chemotherapy and other medicines, most of which I've been able to have administered at home, or locally in either Utica or Rome. The part that's killing me though, is I've been too run down to work , so I had to move from Utica with the band and the majority of my friends back to Rome with my mom.*
>
> *Now don't get me wrong- I LOVE being with my family and seeing my brothers and being able to see them grow up and accomplish things that I was missing being in Utica, but now I'm*

kinda stuck in the middle.

When I was in Utica, I had lost touch with my friends from home since I didn't have a means to travel back to Camden as much and see everyone. Now, I'm in Rome and I'm still without a vehicle and I don't even have my Utica friends anymore, and STILL can't go to see my Camden friends.

But that's why I'm writing this. I get seasonal depression as it is, but that combined with the events of the past 5 months (So much treatment, without being around my peers) has just got me down, and kicked me while I was down, and continues to kick me every time I try to get up. However there are a handful of friends who have made an effort to make sure that they at the LEAST keep in touch with me and give a call here and there to make sure I'm not ready to jump off the roof (ha-ha).

So part of this blog is to thank everyone who hasn't given up on me and the other half is to open the doors to ANYONE who wants to know what's going on with me or any details or anything like that, please don't feel like you're bothering me. I'm a pretty open book and have been since this whole thing started.

Speaking of; there's good news and bad news on that. May 28th of this year will mark my FIVE YEAR survival bench mark. May 28, 2003, I was diagnosed and 5 years later I'm still kickin'.

The downside to that is that my Doctors

have informed me that from here on out my treatments will be handled as a "chronic illness", similar to a diabetic, in that we're working on a day to day basis to keep things where they are. What this means is basically, they don't have a cure, and they don't see one in sight. So we're just gonna try to slow the monster down by throwing things in its path while we wait for a cure for cancer, as cliché as that's become.

I've thought about possibly enrolling in clinical trials at the National Institute of Health, in Bethesda, Maryland, to try new up and coming medical trials. I've also thought about looking into the Cancer Centers of America in Texas. I'm just not happy with the thought that I have this time bomb inside of me and no one knows how to disable it.

Ok, this got long, quick, so I guess the biggest point of this was to thank everyone who has been there for me, and to ask for your continued support....lord knows I need it now possibly more than I ever have...

I love you guys,
Love
JayCW

During this time, February-March, he saw Dr. Desai at Faxton-St. Luke's Hospital in Utica. He was doing another outpatient chemo treatment with him, but we had a lot more confidence in his ability to treat him than the last time he did local infusions. Dr. Desai worked very closely with Dr. Khorana, and came highly recommended locally.

He was very compassionate, and kind to Jason. But, the treatment was not successful, and we were still grasping at straws trying to find something to work for him.

In March, 2008, we took up a collection in the family, and sent Jason on a two week vacation to Florida to stay with my sister and her family. He had the time of his life! Even though he had to take it easier than he would have liked, he said over and over how it was the best time he ever had. It was the first real vacation he had ever been on, other than with the family, where he had money, was in a paradise climate, and could do pretty much whatever he wanted, other than being a little limited because of the trouble he had with fatigue and the breathing difficulties. I was so glad he got to do that. I was worried sick about him, but I had to believe it was what he was supposed to be doing. I know now that it absolutely was.

My sister sent me this story about his trip.....

Jason arrived for his vacation on Easter Sunday. We were all so happy to have him come because he didn't get to visit when the rest of the family came at Thanksgiving. I knew that he wasn't feeling well, but really if I am honest with myself, I was in denial that it was as serious as it was. We were just so excited to be able to spend some time with him. He was dressed so sharp in his sport coat and jeans when he got here. We were waiting to have dinner until he arrived and it took him a little while to come to the table. I didn't know until later that he was having such a difficult time breathing and that sometimes he had panic attacks. I'm sure that the trip and getting settled was about all he could handle for that day, but he came and sat with us at the table even though he really didn't have any appetite.

When he came to the table, I remember how happy he was to be with us, and we had a wonderful dinner with laughs and funny stories about the people he had met while traveling. The girls were filling him in on all the plans they were making for the week and he must have said ten times how glad he was that he came. The girls will fill you in on some of their escapades. (I'm sure I only know the details they wanted me to know at the time!!)

He loved the house and pool and especially the back yard where we had a hammock set up under the trees. He would go out there and sway in the hammock several times throughout the days. I now know that when he felt a panic attack coming, this spot calmed him down. I wish that I had known it then. We actually built "Jason's Beach" in our backyard. Dave will tell you about that.

The whole time that he was with us, he was so uplifting. I can't imagine not being angry with the world and everyone in it if I had been in his situation. He actually was talking to me about several people he was worried about because of different things they were going through. He was trying to come up with ways to help them. That was Jay.

When it came time for him to leave to fly to Boston, none of us wanted him to go. He was cheering at the hockey games (almost got into a fight), making us laugh with his stories, and even the girls' friends that he just met were almost mesmerized by him. I remember all of them wishing he could stay.

He was so excited about making the demo disc with the Blueprint. He was telling us how everything came together to make this CD, and couldn't wait to get there. We talked to Jay a few times while he was there and he was thrilled with how things were coming together, but he was cold after being so warm in Florida.

One of the funniest stories he told us when he came home, was about one of the "21st Birthday Parties" he went to for one of Julie and Jessica's friends. Apparently, he was feeling pretty run down, and having a hard time getting his strength and spirits up to go to the party. He called his "best" friend, Dan Reidy, and told him of his dilemma. I can only imagine the look on Dan's face on the other end of the phone.

"OK, Jay, let me get this straight. You are in Florida. The weather is perfect. You have money in your pocket. You were invited to go in a stretch excursion limo with twenty-five 21 yr. old girls to celebrate one of their 21st birthdays; and, you are calling me to 'Talk you into it??' Dude! C'mon!"

Jay said he was like, "Ok, man. Thanks a lot!"

His last day in Florida was spent with my niece, Jessica, on a quiet beach on the causeway to Honeymoon Island State Park. They decided to just take it easy and chill before he had to go back early the next morning. Of course, the best laid plans…..here is Jessica's version of what happened on that not so quiet day!

73

It was a quiet Monday on the Dunedin Causeway. It was just after midday, the sun was hot and directly overhead, and the waters of the Gulf of Mexico practically stood still. All the boaters and jet skiers had packed it up till the next weekend; there was nothing going on at all; in fact the only thing going on at all on this particular day was a senior s bike event. So lucky for Jay and I, there were handfuls of senior citizens in spandex randomly riding up and down the sidewalks at any given time. Now, for those of you who don't know, the Dunedin causeway itself is about 100 yards wide with a road in the middle, it stretches nearly two miles long on each side, and at the very end of it is the entrance to Honeymoon Island State Park. I had been to that causeway at least a hundred times since I moved from New York - it's my favorite spot in all of Florida; and I thought Jay would enjoy the warmth, peace, and sunshine of the Gulf of Mexico on his last day of vacation before he headed off to Boston to record with the Band.

Jay and I were both pretty tired, because in the last week we had been in a stretch excursion limo with a twenty- five person entourage, been to reggae night at Red Fish Blue Fish, ladies night in Palm Harbor, channel side in down town Tampa, had celebrated two twenty-first birthdays, gone to the horse track, and watched DJ play the state championship at the St. Pete Times forum, where we almost had to fight a half dozen hockey moms. Not to mention, Julie had taken Jay to every shopping mall and plaza within a thirty mile radius, at least twice!! Jay had a six am flight the

*next day for Boston, and I had to work that night.
We were burnt out, and just looking to relax and
unwind.*

*At the time, I had a 1997 jeep wrangler.
On that day, Jay and I had taken the doors off, put
the top down, took a long cruise along the sand,
and picked a nice quiet spot to spend the day.
There was no one near us for at least 30 feet on
each side, we had picked a location close to the
bathrooms, yet far enough away where we
wouldn't be bothered by any fishing lines in case
we wanted to go for a swim and cool off. We
parked the jeep, turned up the radio, laid out our
towels, and took turns with the lotion. I grabbed
my SPF4 banana boat, and Jay helped so I didn't
have crazy tan lines all over my back; and then
Jay grabbed his SPF 45 baby, and we covered his
already bright pink body head to toe!! We were
just chillin', listening to the radio, and laughing at
all of the highlights from the past week.*

*All of a sudden we heard sirens; we both
glanced over expecting to see some sorry soul get a
speeding ticket. We looked directly behind us and
saw some disturbed man in a truck, and a few too
many cop cars for the ordinary traffic stop. Then,
we heard the guy who got pulled over shouting
back and forth out the window with law
enforcement. Naturally, Jay and I stand up trying
to get a closer look when we see a shot gun pointed
directly at us! I hit the sand, I couldn't believe it.
I looked over and noticed Jay was right there on
the side of the Jeep, saying, "Jess you gotta see
this! I need my phone to take a picture!" We
were probably stuck right behind the shooter for*

75

about twenty minutes; but, lucky for us, there was a big 300 lb Mexican guy on vacation parked right next to us with a white construction van. We took cover behind the van with a few other people for about a half hour when cops with shields started escorting people a safer distance away from the shooter.

When this thing started, Jay and I were less than 15 yards away from the guy with the gun. By the end of this thing, it was a 6-7 hour standoff, over 30 cop cars and sheriff cars had shown up, a coast guard helicopter, news helicopters, and two sheriff boats. The boats dropped off a half dozen sharp shooters in camo-gear; of course when Jay and I saw the boats, we thought that they were rescue boats sent here to save us, or at least bring food! Throughout that afternoon, we were pushed further and further down the causeway towards the island by police barricades, but along the way we had quite the adventure and even made some friends.

I remember shortly after we were escorted away from the white van, Jay was seeking some shade, and I had managed to wander off into some brush while trying to get a closer look at the standoff. Of course, running around barefoot, I got a sliver in the bottom of my foot . Jay had worked his charm on some old ladies in spandex, and they gave us some water bottles and tweezers, and Jay got my sliver out. Next we walked down by the bridge and saw a few guys our age, which meant Jay and I finally found the beer! And let me tell you, at this point of the day, it was better than finding gold. Next we just kind of walked

*around aimlessly , chit chatting, and making sure
everything was as good as it could be. At one
point, Jay witnessed a girl having a nicotine fit,
and managed to find her a cigarette, and in return
we got some peanuts off some fisherman. Around
this time Jay had adopted my cell as his, since he
didn't grab his as he was too distracted with the
shooter when we ran behind the Mexican man's
van. So he was updating all of Palm Harbor on
the status from our side of the island. However, I
really think by this time in the day, Jay just wanted
to call the guy in the truck and tell him to pull the
friggin' trigger!*

*We spotted this ice cream truck wicked
early in the standoff. We, along with several
others, kept harassing the poor guy for free ice
cream, but it wasn't until the 5th hour that the ice
cream man actually opened up the back of the
truck for a free for all!! I noticed that Jay had
grabbed several ice creams. Knowing it's not
Jay's character to be greedy, I didn't say anything.
We started walking down the causeway, when I
looked over and noticed Jay had taken the ice
cream as a last way to meet every last blonde in the
state! Grinning ear to ear, he just started passing
out ice cream sandwiches to everyone as we
walked back over the bridge.*

*We made friends with this one particular
guy in a canoe. After hours in the sun, Jay was
turning into a bald headed lobster! The guy let us
chill in his truck throughout the day and gave us
Gatorades and sunscreen. The guy ended up
working for the St. Pete Times, and because of the
standoff he couldn't make it into work that night,*

so he called in the story from his truck. Lucky for him, he met the two witnesses from the beginning of the standoff! Jay and I felt like celebrities at this point; we each talked to the newspaper and told him what happened and what we had witnessed thus far.

Later on that night we finally made it home, and my cell rang. Jay, who became attached to it like it was his own, answered it. It was my friend Moe whose sister's limo we had been in a couple nights earlier. Jay starts telling Moe how some jackass tried ruining his last day of vacation and how he wanted to shoot him in the head himself! Moe goes "Oh yeah, well that jack ass is my uncle!" Ha ha ha.

Funny thing is, about a week ago I was visiting Moe who is now 8 months pregnant, and I was watching TV on the couch with her and some random family member. After I left her house, she texted me. "By the way, you just met my Uncle Ricky!!"

Now that I look back, I wish I had thanked Uncle Ricky for giving me a whole day to spend with my cousin. We were barefoot with absolutely nothing but our swim suits the day of the standoff, but that's all we really needed to have one hell of a day at the beach!

I am thankful that Uncle Ricky was sick in the head that day. It was a crazy week, and Jay and I hadn't really gotten a chance to just sit and talk. I think the last time that Jay and I had been that open in conversations like we were that day, must have been when we were kids playing outside with his remote control cars in Camden and on Sam Street at Grandma's. That day, it was just the two of us, and neither one of us is ever short of words. We must have talked about everything and then everything! It makes me laugh now. I know at one point, we had just scored some snacks off an old lady, and were sitting on the bridge with our feet dangled over the Gulf, and I remember Jay was teaching me how to hunt! Mind you, I have never been hunting a day in my life! But if I had to do it that day, I am sure we would have been just fine. In return, I remember explaining to Jay the importance of the upcoming election, and how I got grandma to volunteer for Rudy! Ha ha.

I worry a lot about the little things, but with Jay, nothing ever seems too big to handle. At one point during that week that Jay visited, I had what I considered to be a life threatening problem at the time. I failed to request transcripts from undergrad, and Jay was the poor soul who had to calm me down, fix the printer, and help mail out all my law applications.

After spending time with Jay, it makes me put a lot of things in better perspective. I know one thing; the most important thing in life is family. At the time of this story, I didn't understand why it had happened to us. I mean the causeway is miles long, and the day started off as a quiet and boring Monday. I now know why God held Jay and I hostage that day. It took me a while to get it together to write this, mostly because it was the last time I got to hung out with Jay

before he passed. Now every time I go to the
causeway, I see our quiet little spot and smile, and
pick up a shell or two for Jay's beach that we built
at home and place them around his hammock.

*****

When he left Florida, he flew to Boston to finish recording his last CD with his band. The band said he was incredible - struggling through each take, and having to rest after each one. He loved that band, and wanted to make sure that their CD was finished and done right.

He got back home the first week of April. On April 15th he had another CT scan done and the results were devastating. According to the report, almost all of the lesions on his lungs had grown in size since the January scan - some had more than doubled.

Jason sent out an email on April 19th to update his family and friends on his condition. He was still being so strong and controlled, I'm sure because he was trying to keep everyone else calm. This is what he sent out:

Subject: Long Health Update:

Well, I'm going to try to make this a coverall so maybe it's the first you've heard of things or maybe you just needed to fill in the blanks a little bit, but either way here goes...

This past Tuesday (April 15th) I had my most recent CT scan. Friday (April 18th) I received the results from that scan. (I have attached the actual files, if you're familiar at all with reading scan

*dictations...or reading, period I guess ha-ha).
Basically what the scan showed was that all the
major tumors and most of the rest of them for that
matter have at LEAST doubled in size since
January 11th. Some are worse than others, IE-
The one on the outside of my lower left lung has
grown to the point where I can feel a sharp pain
when I breathe, walk, lay down, sit up....more or
less all the time. I've been prescribed Fentanyl
patches though, to help deal with the pain, and so
far I've been managing it really well.*

*However, the fact remains that this is:
1) the worst condition I've been in since I
was diagnosed and
2) the fastest the disease has spread over
the shortest period of time. So, yeah, it's pretty
scary.*

*What's worse is that when we asked them
what the next step was, they informed me that I
was "out of steps." When the cancer returned
after my first (and last) resection surgery, they told
me that I wouldn't be eligible for further surgery
in the future because it would cause more damage
than good. I've tried every type of medically
approved Chemotherapy or non-chemo oral pill
that they have for my type of cancer. Any further
doses of radiation therapy to my lungs might cause
the collapse of a lung, or cause even more
breathing problems. I am currently on two inhaler
medicines (Advair, Albuterol) to control the
shortness of breath and coughing fits that I
experience when doing tasks that, in my mind, I
feel I should be able to do without restriction.*

So, that being said... I have to call Roswell Park Cancer Center in Buffalo, NY to attempt to enroll in their clinical trials. They have a program called "Phase 1" which means that they will be administering medications that have not previously been tested, and whose results are unknown. It's roulette, only it's generally over the course of 4-6 weeks at a time.

I will also be contacting Sloan-Kettering in NYC, with the same questions. Each hospital will ask me a series of questions, as well as looking at my medical charts and see if I'm what they need for their studies.

So, I mean, it's not good news, but I'm gonna try (as always) to make the best of it...although, admittedly a bit more pessimistic this time, I'm still not down and out, and, therefore, I'm gonna keep moving forward and looking for answers where ever they may be. Right now, we're checking Buffalo.

If anyone has any questions or anything, lemme know...please feel free to ask I'm more than open to talk about this whole thing.

Thanks for listening guys, love and miss you all!
Love
Jay

Jason and I had started looking at other options. His aunt in Texas had contacted a doctor at the University of Texas Health Science Center who thought they might be able to help him, based on the limited information they had.

We had asked Strong to forward any necessary information they may need, but for some reason, they seemed to be dragging their feet. It was very strange, because for five years, they had been there for us every step of the way, going out of their way to make things easier for us. Now, it seemed like we couldn't even get them to return phone calls.

In the meantime, Jason was getting worse every day. He was on Fentanyl patches for pain, plus pretty much unlimited Oxycodone pills. One day, he was complaining about the pain in his lower left back. He was saying he felt something, so I looked at his back and I couldn't believe what I was seeing. There was a bulge on his back in the spot where one of the biggest, fastest growing tumors was. It was limiting his breathing and extremely painful. We called Dr. Khorana's office and they gave us an appointment immediately with Dr. Katz, to see if he could do radiation on the sight, just to try to slow down the growth of the tumor. When we arrived and he examined Jay, he said the problem was that there was fluid building up in the lining of the lung, between the outside of the lung, and one of the tumors that was growing. He decided to do a thoracentesis to relieve some of the fluid. They would insert a tube into the lining of his lung and drain the fluid.

On April 22nd, 2008, they did the first procedure and removed a liter and a half of fluid. Then they did ten more rounds of radiation to the tumor on the lower left lung. They did one more thoracentesis, and removed another liter and a half two weeks later.

I remember on one of our rides home from the treatments, Jason noticed two horses that were in a field along side the thruway. One of the horses was laying down. It was strange, because neither of us could remember ever seeing a horse laying down like that in the middle of the day. Plus, the other horse was just standing over him. Jay was so concerned he called Caitlyn Lalonde and asked her if it was normal. This is her recollection of Jay's experience with horses, and him calling her that day:

So Jason went to school with my cousins and I met him when I was little, however, several years went by before I saw him again. The first time we re-connected was at the Grape n Grog on Memorial Day in 2005. We were just chatting while we cleaned up, and somehow horses came up in the conversation. I told Jay that I had been riding since I was 4, and that we had 35 horses at my house. The look on his face was priceless. I came to know that face very well. "The classic Jay face." I'm pretty sure everyone can identify with what I am talking about. So a few weeks went by. I saw him more frequently on the weekends, and we started talking more and more, and eventually we grew to be great friends. There was just something about him that made me open up to him. I am sure everyone who had the pleasure to know Jay, can relate to that.

We were out one night during the week, and there were very many people out, so Jay decided he was going to teach me some pool skills. After about an hour of helping me out, he decided we would play a game of pool. Now, I am horrible at pool, so jokingly I made a bet with him that if I won, he would have to come to my house and ride a horse. He laughed and agreed. He was pretty confident in winning, so at the time he didn't seem to mind. That was until he sunk the 8 ball in by mistake! I just looked at him and then.....I got "The Classic Jay Face" again. He was speechless.

A few days later, Jay ended up coming down to ride. All he said to me was, "Cait, please don't let me fall off." I insisted that I wouldn't, but for some reason, he didn't really believe me. So after a few minutes of convincing him the horse wouldn't hurt him, he finally got on. He was obviously pretty nervous at first, but eventually he chilled out, and believe it or not, he was pretty good! We put the horse back, and he fed him treats. After that he made me go around outside and tell him every horse's name and he gave each one a treat. After that he always asked about the horses and said he wanted to come back. He came a few times to watch me ride, but I left at the end of August to go to school, so his barn visits stopped.

He came a few more times the next summer to see the horses. Our friendship grew really close again, and we had some great times that summer. I went back to Tennessee for school, and ended up moving back home to go to school in January.
You bet that my first night home, I went to go see Jay play. We grew apart a little bit again, but he was always a phone call away. I don't think that there is one time that he didn't pick up the phone when I called. He always loved to talk. Ha, that's an understatement! However, he always had some sort of advice.

Through all of our conversations though, the most prominent line I can remember was

"Cait, Just don't lose who you are. Make sure you take care of you first & don't lose touch with the things you love." I asked him what he meant and he told me that he didn't know much about the horses, but he did know that he hadn't ever seen a person happier than me, when I was riding.

Jay and I kept in touch. It got kind of difficult sometimes when I was busy with school, and he was not feeling the best, but we did the best we could. This past spring I would talk to him as often as time allowed. We had a set time once a week that we would call and talk, but most of the time I ended up calling him and waking him up. He never seemed to mind. He told me when he was better he wanted to come to the barn again and see the horses. When times were really tough, we would joke around about it, and he was all excited to come back.

However, sometimes I would get random phone calls from Jay. The last random call I got from him, was when he was on his way back from Rochester and he saw a horse in the field and it was laying down. He was all freaked out that it shouldn't be laying like that, and he asked me about a million questions. I answered them, and of course laughed the whole time. That was Jay, though. Concerned about everything and everyone.

Ironic enough, I was bringing the horse that Jay rode into the barn when I received the call that he had passed away. Looking back on the memories now make me smile. He was such a wonderful person. Every time I go in the show ring now I know I'll be okay, and I'll do well, because I have a very special person riding with me on my shoulder. There's not much more I can ask for.

Caitlyn Lalonde

Caitlyn sent me this email a week or so after the first one:

Hello Tammy!

I have been thinking more and more about Jason lately (if that is possible...) and after writing that story, I have been thinking about doing a "Freestyle Jumping Course" in memory of Jason. It would be like a 4 minute presentation I would do on horseback to music. I would be jumping and doing other things. I had thought about doing it to "Let It Be." I just wanted to check with you and see what you thought :-) I will definitely have it videotaped, and can send it on :-) Let me know what you think!

Thanks so much!
Caitlyn

I told her he would love that!

The "Let It Be" reference was significant because Gary Johnson played it at the funeral service. The reason we chose that song was because of this email he sent out a few weeks before. Again, I think it was all part of "checking things off the bucket list".

--- On Fri, 5/9/08, Jason Wilhelm wrote:

I finally found ...

The Beatles...

"And when the broken hearted people
Living in the world agree,
There will be an answer, let it be.
For though they may be parted there is
Still a chance that they will see
There will be an answer, let it be."

He had said to Gary that he "Found the Beatles like some people find God." I had that verse of *Let It Be* inscribed on the back of his monument.........even though they screwed up the words - but that is a later story!

It was around this time that we started planning the party at Lake Delta for his "Five Year Survival Anniversary." It was even more important now, because the situation had become so dire so quickly. It was what kept him focused and moving forward for the whole month of May.

We ordered white bracelets like the Live Strong bracelets that just had "JAYCW" imprinted on them. He was going to give them out at the party to all of his friends and family.

JayCW was how he would sign his name, and what he had as his personal "logo" on his MySpace and Facebook pages. At some point, all of his friends started putting his signature on their sites, and it just spread all over the internet. It was almost like an unspoken prayer for him. He was so moved by that, that he told everyone. He sent out this email to Aunt Michelle.

To: Michelle Wilhelm (May 8, 2008 8:30pm)
Subject:

So, all my friends have this JAYCW logo in their profiles and away messages and it's just everywhere... I think my mom is having wristbands made up that are just simple white bands with JAYCW on them.. that's how I sign my name, especially at shows with younger kids who actually wanted autographs ha-ha.. and lots of friends have put that in their profiles and spread it around online for me without me even asking....it's a pretty special feeling...but I'll set some aside for the family, then the rest I'll give out at the party.. I'll have to make sure to mail some or bring some with me, depending on what the case ends up being....

We booked a pavilion at Lake Delta for May 31st because the 28th is 5 years since I was diagnosed and we're just gonna throw this monster party there (assuming I'm home then, and if not then whatever - we'll postpone it) but that should be fun...I'll make sure to take a lot of pictures because its gonna be all my friends, my moms friends, all the family and just everyone in the area basically so I have something positive to look forward to.

During these radiation visits, at the beginning of May, we went to talk to Dr. Khorana, and see why he was not cooperating with the doctor in Texas who wanted to review Jason's charts, and had requested information.

We didn't have an appointment, but we went to the Cancer Center after one of his radiation treatments, and asked to speak to Lisa McNiece. We told her what was going on with Jay, and that we were concerned because Dr. Khorana hadn't responded to the requests for the records. She told us that the Cancer Center had been moving into a new wing the previous few weeks and things were chaotic. Then, she told us to wait in the waiting room, and went to talk to Dr. Khorana. She came back, and said that he wanted to talk to us, and brought us into an exam room.

He explained to us that he wasn't sure that the hospital in Texas was such a good idea. The doctor wasn't an oncologist, he was a pathologist. There was not really any reason to think that he would have a treatment available that would help Jason's situation. Jason told him he wanted to try anyway, and he agreed to send whatever information they needed.

Then, Jason asked him the question we had not asked in the entire five years. He wanted to know, if we didn't find another avenue, how long he had. Khorana looked at him, and said, "Maybe a few months."

Months??? That was the first week of May. We left the office and I remember Jason didn't say anything. He didn't cry, or react in any way. I immediately started crying - tears just poured out of my eyes. We walked quietly to our car, and my phone rang right when we reached the car. Jason got in, and I stayed out and answered the phone. It was Jason's Aunt Michelle. She was the one who had the contact with the doctor in Houston. She was calling to follow up, to see if we had contacted Strong for information yet. I blurted out the news. "They just said he has a few months!" I'm sorry, Michelle - you must have felt totally blindsided!

I tried to get back in control before I got into the car. We drove the entire two hours without saying anything. I remember I just had tears running down my face the whole time.

I stayed home with him from then on. I wanted to try to help him to stay focused and not get depressed. Not that it wasn't warranted - I think that would be on top of the list of justifiable depression. But I kept trying to keep him up and doing things. He would get so mad at me for just making stuff up for us to do. But, he was so cooperative!

I think the best thing we ever did was to plan the party at Lake Delta. It gave him something to look forward to, and kept him focused on positive things for the whole month.

I remember the day we went to Camden and met up with Diane Hollibaugh and Debbie Kent and spent a couple of hours there just catching up with them. Diane was Jason's good friend, Chad's mother, and Debbie was a good friend who was also battling cancer, but more importantly, had formed a bond with Jason over the years. It took a while to get Debbie's email story, but I couldn't imagine finishing the book without it.

Debbie Kent:

When it comes to Jason - I don't remember there ever being a beginning, like when was the first time I met him? It actually feels like I always knew him. But I think that was one of the qualities I loved most about Jay. He was just an ordinary guy but with an extra-ordinary compassion for others. I do remember, however, our sharing a

bond because of cancer. It's kind of a nasty thing
to form a bond over, but that's just the way it was.
Jay and I both learned how to deal with cancer,
each in our own way, but whenever we saw each
other I felt 'one' with him. After the hello's and
hugs we would say just a few things about what we
were going through, but then it didn't take long at
all before we were talking about the happy things
in life......and then I wouldn't see him again for
some time. But when I did, we just sort of picked
up where we left off; it was just like we saw each
other everyday. That's the way it went until the
sad rumors started ... then I spent some time with
him, took a few pictures of him with his mom ...
but before I knew it ... I was helping to plan how
we would say good bye.... That's the part that
seems unreal. Even though I won't run into Jay in
this world anymore, there are so many times when
I "run into" him in my heart and soul.
Thanks Jay for keeping it 'real' for me, and
reminding me of all the happy things we can find
in each other ... just like we did.
Peace, Debbie Kent

We were reminiscing about everything from the
first time Tom Fanning saw Jason playing with Chad and
remarked to Diane about him being one of the smartest kids
he ever taught - to Jason and Chad getting caught on the
roof of my house at 2am because they thought they could
get away with it. I can't even remember the excuse they
used for being up there.

Mario Hollibaugh sent Jason this message on his
MySpace after that visit.

*Hey man! My mom said you stopped in the other day to see her and say 'hi'. Just got me to thinking about it today cuz I called her and even on Mother's Day some people didn't call or say 'hi' or send her a card or anything, but you went to see her. She sounded so happy on the phone about it. I just wanted to say what's up to ya, and see what's new and exciting back in ol' York, and say thank you for making my mother's day. So, thanks man ^^*

Mario

He truly loved Diane and was so glad I "made" him go that day. Diane and Debbie always held such a special place in his heart. Truth be told, Diane Hollibaugh is responsible for Jason getting his first drum set! They were 12, and he and Chad were on a drum kick. They had both decided they wanted to be drummers, and asked for drums for Christmas.

I remember talking to Diane about it, and she was the one who told me that he actually had a talent - she wasn't sure about Chad, (sorry, Chad), but she thought Jason might really be serious about learning the drums. All I could think of was the noise! But, on her advice, Bob and I bought Jason his first drum set for Christmas that year - the year he turned 13.

That was one of my favorite Christmases. Jason and Tommy actually got their first drum sets the same year. Tommy was just turning two, and Joey was only 6 months old. We bought Tom an "all-in-one" plastic drum set with plastic drum sticks with round balls on the end. He carried them everywhere.

Jason and Erin got up very early and were down in

the living room. They were trying to wake up while opening their stockings. After about 20 minutes or so, Erin went into the kitchen to get a drink. She immediately came back in the living room and said to him, "Jay, you need to get a drink."

Without looking at her, said, "No, I don't need a drink."

She said, "Jay - YOU NEED TO GET A DRINK! NOW!"

It still took him a minute, then finally he said, "Wait, is there something in the kitchen!?!" He ran to the kitchen still holding the orange he was peeling. Bob and I were in there waiting with the camera, next to the new Ludwig drum set that was set up in the kitchen. He stopped dead in his tracks when he saw it.

"Holy SHIT!" he blurted out!

"JASON!" I yelled! "Shame! Shame!"

"SORRY! SORRY!" was all he could say. It was so funny. He threw his orange away and sat down and started playing. The rest is history. He worked at it and got better and better. He joined the fife and drum corps with Randy Waterman. It was one of the most rewarding things he had in his life. He absolutely loved playing the drums and performing with his bands.

He also loved it that Thomas was a drummer, and he loved being his mentor. However, I remember that their first interaction as drummers was Jason teasing Tom when he got up in the morning.

"Hey, Tommy! You got a new drum set from Santa? Wow! Hey, come see mine in the kitchen - sucker!" Boy, he was such a brat!

*****

The other thing he did during that May was to finally get a tattoo. He had talked about it for at least three or four years. He had his good friend, Katie Ramsden working on a design, and he had all kinds of ideas on what he wanted to do. He definitely wanted to make sure whatever it ended up being, it reflected his personality, his struggle with this dreaded disease, and something that would always remind him to find the best in every situation because you just never know. When he finally got it, it really turned out beautiful! He sent out this email to his family.

Subject: Checking things off the bucket list!
Date: Saturday, May 17, 2008, 7:01 PM

I know that everyone's going to have mixed feelings about this....I've only showed Aunt Michelle (which means the whole family probably saw it down there) but for everyone else....I got my first Tattoo on Friday afternoon.

You can download the pictures, but to give a little background, it's a red rose, with a banner with the date May 28th, 2003. That's the date I was diagnosed with cancer. I'm debating having the very bottom tip of the stem sort of turn into a small line of medical tubing and "into my wrist" the way an IV would look....I like the idea because either way it works...if it's a needle giving medicine, it's administering the content of the Rose, which a red

95

rose symbolizes love....or if it's interpreted as a blood DRAW where it was coming OUT, it would appear that my blood is so full of love and sincerity that it blossomed a rose...I just don't want it looked at morbidly is my only problem...

Ok enough talking, onto to the pictures!!
Hope you like it, because I am in LOVE with it!
News coming this week I hope about the next step also!

Love always,
Jay
The guy with the new tattoo!

And he absolutely was in love with it. He designed it himself with the woman at the tattoo parlor, and it came out beautiful! He spent hours taking pictures and making sure everyone he knew saw it.

So, needless to say, the weeks following that bleak prognosis flew by before we knew it. Jason was having more and more problems breathing, but he was trying so hard to stay positive. One night, he was again having the pain and trouble with the fluid on his lungs. I brought him to the ER at Faxton-St Luke's and after a long night of waiting, they admitted him.

The staff at the hospital was very attentive to him and accommodating to me as well. They let me stay with him in the room. I honestly didn't even realize it at the time, but he was so bad off at that point, they let me stay because they knew he was close to the end. It was then that he really started to get scared and I did, too. My mother was there, of course, but I knew that there was no way she would be strong enough to help me with what I feared was

96

ahead.

Jason started having these attacks where he would not be able to breathe, and he would panic and they would have to give him a shot - I think it was morphine - to calm him down again. After a particularly bad attack, I called Cheri and I lost it. I asked her to come up, because I knew my mother wouldn't be able to help me, and I wouldn't be much help to her, either. After I hung up and got a grip, I had second thoughts. I decided I was panicking and I sent her a txt saying no need to jump the gun, maybe we should wait until the next morning and see how things were going. It was too late. She had already booked the flight. She was there the next day. This is how she remembers that awful night....

I now want to talk about the night that Jay went into the hospital. I was getting text updates from my sister and I clearly remember her sending me a text about how worried she was. I sent her one back that said whenever you want me to come just tell me. In about 2 seconds, my phone rang and when I answered it was her sobbing. She said, " I can't do this alone and Mom can't help me." It was at this moment that it all became real to me. She was talking about watching her son die and it came crashing down on me like a ton of bricks. We booked the flight out and the next morning I was on my way to Rome.

I remember DJ asking "What are you doing?"
I said' "I am going to help Aunt Tammy and Grandma."
And his answer to me was, "Who is going to help you?"

97

The next morning when I walked into the hospital room I remember how tired Jay looked from just 6 weeks ago. He had lost weight and looked so pale. Tammy was just glad to have me there. We talked and laughed and Jay told me all about Boston. I still think that I was in denial, because I no way thought that he would be gone in a little over a week.

We talked about the big 5 year party and he was so excited about all his friends coming to it from all over the country. I really hadn't met any of his friends at this point but I was about to. They came one after another for the next five days. I specifically remember Nick, Eric, Gary and Dan. There were many more, though.

I remember saying to him, "Listen, all you have to do is pull on your ear when you want peace and quiet, and I will clear the room for you!" Never once did he do it!

I came to love those kids over that week. They were so thoughtful and caring and funny and loving to him. The only time that I saw him even a little sad is one time when we were talking about the party, he was so upset that he might have to go in a wheel chair. It broke both of our hearts to see him in tears, and I actually had to leave the room because I didn't want him to see me break down. I had a massive melt down in the rest room across the hall. It probably didn't help that Tammy and I were both reading the Last Lecture that Aunt Jan had recommended. Mom was in and out throughout the week, and she was having a really hard time.

*****

When Jason would have trouble breathing and he would go into these panic attacks. I would have to literally talk him out of it, and help him to think of something that would calm him down. He came up with the hammock in my sister's back yard in Florida. When he was on vacation at the end of March, he said his favorite spot was in the hammock in the back yard. So, when he would have trouble breathing, and start to panic, he would imagine himself in the hammock, rocking back and forth, and bring his attack under control. It became quite a joke with us at the hospital.

Because of this, my sister and brother-in-law created a memorial in their back yard for Jason. This is Dave's story about "Jason's Beach".

..........Upon my wife's return from Jason's bedside with her sister Tammy over this past Memorial weekend, Cheri started to tell me some of the stories that Jason was experiencing. One of the stories was when Jason was sleeping quietly trying to hold off some of the anxiety attacks that he would get.

With eyes closed and peacefully resting, Jay all of a sudden flinched. When asked what happened, Jay replied... "I was dreaming I was at Aunt Cheri's house in the back yard on her hammock resting and I just fell off the hammock!" It was there on the hammock that Jay said he was at peace just relaxing.
At the funeral for Jay as I was hugging

Tammy. She had told me the story about the hammock. At that split second I thought......
"What better way to always remember Jay's visit?" I told Tammy I would build a memorial beach in my back yard and call it "JASON'S BEACH" with the focal point being a permanent hammock that Jay slept in as the center piece.

Upon returning home from the funeral, I started researching how and where I would put it. I then cleared out a 500 square foot section in the back corner of my yard. I ordered five tons of beach sand and away we went. It took about two months to complete and for those who do not know how hot it is in Florida, come down in June and July. It had to be 99 degrees with 100% humidity every day when Cheri, the kids, and I worked on hand carting the sand from the front of our house to the beach in the back.

Every weekend I would search for special pieces to make the beach perfect. I would come across an old oar and then some fishing nets for the back fence. I found a very old anchor and some worn buoys. I have some deadwood, sea grass, sea gulls and actual shells from Honeymoon Island State Park on the Gulf of Mexico. After adding a skim board and Tiki torches, I thought we should add some old Adirondack chairs I found on e-bay from California. We then put in a fireplace pit sunk in the sand for some night time bonfires.

Finally, I cut and hand painted hanging destination arrows behind the hammock - complete with mile markers - to Rome, Buffalo,

Giants Stadium, Fenway Park and for
Jay…. Yankee Stadium. A specially made sign,
"JASON'S BEACH" hangs behind the hammock.

Funny how every day and night sweating,
almost passing out from the heat, many times I
would just say to myself…… "Remember why you
are doing this." It was for Jay - and especially
for Tammy. I don't know if I ever put more
thought and sweat into a project like this before.

It is now complete. On weekends I rake the
sand and blow the leaves off of it. We have
bonfires and make s'mores. We have a beer or
two, and sit quietly next to the hammock where
Jay peacefully rested.

*****

After being in the hospital for almost a week, they started talking about sending him home. My sister and my mother were trying to convince me to have a hospital bed put in the downstairs bedroom for him. I was afraid that if we did that, Jason would give up and think we had given up. I was still convinced that we had more time. I knew he couldn't do the stairs, so I called Dan Reidy and he came over with a friend of theirs and moved Jason's bedroom furniture downstairs to set up in the spare bedroom. I remember Dr. Desai mentioned Hospice the day before Jay was discharged. He asked if he had a DNR signed, or if we had talked about his wishes. I told him we would talk about all that when we got home. Certainly there was plenty of time to worry about those things when he got closer - when we were ready.

Another new 'friend' of Jason's we met that week

was Christina Elacqua. She is a nursing student at the hospital, and she was assigned to the Oncology floor for the last two or three days that Jason was there. I kept seeing these posted messages from her on Jason's Facebook page, and she kept saying over and over how much he had influenced her life in just those short days when she got to spend time with him. They had mutual friends, but were not close. I asked her to send me something for the book.

Christina T. Elacqua

My Jay story..
I was not friends with Jay. I did not know his favorite music artist or what bar he liked to hang out at with his friends. We had mutual friends, so therefore I considered him an acquaintance. We always exchanged greetings with each other and went on our way.

I was coming to the end of my first year of nursing school and for my last clinical rotation I was placed on an oncology floor. My first week was very intimidating, as everyone was extremely ill. I caught a glimpse of Jay's name at the nurses' station and debated whether or not to say 'hi'. Once again, we barely knew each other.

I walked by his room over and over, pretending to be busy. Finally, like someone pushed me on my way, I quietly opened the door leading to his single patient room and I entered. He lay in bed with his music in one hand and his phone in the other. I asked if he remembered who I was, and he did. I walked in his room that day not knowing of the impact that was about to take place in my life and my new nursing career.

102

For two of my days on the floor, I was in and out of Jay's room whenever I was not tending to my own patients. If Jay's shoulder hurt from the position he was lying in, I made sure I rubbed it until he felt somewhat comfortable. When all Jay wanted was red Jell-o, I made sure I marched myself downstairs to the cafeteria and returned with red Jell-o. I am a student nurse. My patients ask and I do. I care for my patients. I treat them with dignity and gentleness. I am a student nurse. It is my job. It is what I love to do.

Jay was different. He was not my patient. He was not my friend. Yet, he touched me on such a deep level that no patient or friend could touch someone. I learned to care so much for Jay. Jay did not need me. He had an assigned nurse. But I was there. I found myself continuously going to visit Jay because of the sense of life that was held in his room. No matter when I walked in, Jay always took his headphones off and talked with me. He was so positive about life. He never spoke of the future. He always talked about the present. He took an interest in my education and asked about my life. He never complained or wanted anyone to go out of their way. He was genuine. Jay was the type of person that a perfect stranger could approach and talk about life with, much as I did. I found myself attracted to Jay's personality and spirituality. On my last day of the week Jay took my hand, squeezed it, and looked me in the eyes. My heart had melted. Melted in a saddened way, for Jay and his friends and family, and a joyful way, that I was able to be touched on such a deep level. Although being weak, his eyes

103

*were piercing with strength and passion of life.
When he spoke, his heart spoke too. Jay's hands
were so gentle to touch and he maintained an aura
of welcoming. I didn't need to know Jay to see
that. It was there in his personality. We
exchanged numbers and I looked forward to
seeing him upon his return home. That week, Jay
passed.*

*Jay was not my patient. He was not a
friend of mine. Yet, Jay became love to me. He
was the sun in clouded skies. He was strength that
over-reigned the weakness. Jay became my
confidant. He became someone I so proudly cared
about. Jay was like a mentor to me. Without
knowing, he showed me that life is something to be
lived to its fullest. As I continue to care for
patients, I will forever remember Jay.*

*****

They discharged him on Friday, May 23rd. We had
to go to a local medical supplier to be set up with an
oxygen system for him to use at the house. We left the
hospital with an oxygen tank, but had no idea how long it
would last. It only lasted for the afternoon.

*(Cheri) The day we actually brought him
home was Friday, I think. Tammy had to get the
oxygen for home, and she got everything situated
for him. Over the weekend, Jay was telling me he
wanted to get a large screen TV for the family with
his tax check, and an Xbox for Andy. I told him
what a great idea it was. He wanted it to be a
surprise so, of course, I didn't
tell Tammy.*

104

That night and Saturday, he seemed to be doing well. Andy and I decided to get the materials to remodel our bathroom, mainly so Jay would be able to take a bath. We had a large walk-in shower, but had always planned on putting in a tub when we redid the bathroom. He had a shower chair but I knew he would love to just take a bath, so that is what we planned. We went to Lowe's and ordered everything and had them deliver it. We weren't sure how it would get done, but at least if we had the supplies there, we could work at it somehow.

I guess I really didn't realize what a hard time Jason was having at that point. I am sure I was in some form of denial. Later, I saw a text message he had sent over the weekend that said he was having a hard time breathing, and another one that said he had to try to keep himself calm, because I wasn't home, and I was the only one who could talk him down. By Sunday I was starting to see how hard it was getting for him, and that he was getting scared as well.

Cheri went home on Monday morning. We had talked a little about it, but there didn't seem to be any reason for her to stay. Jason was home, and stable, for the time being. I had a feeling she was planning on returning for the party the following weekend anyways.

From Cheri:
Monday was Memorial Day so I had to start thinking about getting home. I absolutely wanted to come back for the picnic and I had no doubt that Jay would be at that picnic. I asked Dave to check out flights to come back for the weekend because I was going home on Monday. I thought that I would just surprise everyone by coming back on Saturday.

105

When I was saying goodbye on Monday,
Jay hugged me and said,
"Do you have to go?" I wish that I never left.

After she left, Jason sent a text message to Julie and Jessica saying that their mom was on her way home and that he wasn't ready for her to leave. They joked with him and said he could have her - that they would trade me for her for a while. He laughed and said "Actually, I need them both here." Cheri kept saying she shouldn't have left - that she didn't even know why she thought she had to get back home when she did. But again, fate plays out in mysterious ways, and there is a reason for everything. Sometimes it just takes longer to figure out.

Several months before, Jason had mentioned to me to call Ron Scales to see if he would be interested in helping us do the bathroom. Ron and I actually grew up together, but his son, Bob, and Jason went to school together in Camden. Ron was always a great positive role model for Jason while he was growing up, and he had a lot of respect for him. Ron had experience with home improvement, and Jay thought he would be happy to help if he could. Even though we had talked about calling Ron several times prior to that, I finally called him on Monday afternoon. I told him what we were doing and asked if he would come over and give us advice on where to start. He said he could stop by on Tuesday.

Then, about 5 minutes later, he called back and said he was in Lowe's parking lot just killing time with Karen, and that they could come over then, if we weren't busy. They came right over and he spent half an hour or so talking to Andy while Karen and I did some catching up. Jason was on the phone with his Uncle Kurt who lives in

Switzerland. Jay was having such a hard time talking and breathing, but he hadn't been able to talk to Kurt in a while, so he stayed on the phone probably longer than he should have. Karen said later that she was just watching him try to talk and was heart broken to see him struggling so hard.

Later when he was going to bed, Jason seemed very agitated and uncomfortable. I think he was scared to go to sleep, and, frankly - I was, too. I remember asking him if he wanted me to sleep with him. He just laughed and said, "I really think I'm a little old to need my mother to sleep with me!" I wish I had pulled rank on him.

The next day Ron came over to start on the bathroom. I asked him to send me his story of those last two days. I knew that he would be able to relay the details accurately and eloquently. But first, let me say that I called him to see if we could enlist his help in remodeling our bathroom, and while talking to Karen, when he was in with Andy looking at the project, she ended up THANKING ME for asking Ron to come over to help us. She had been trying to get him out of the store more, and was grateful for the opportunity for him to help us, because it would be good for him. If I was a little less selfish that day, and a little quicker on the draw, I would have offered to help him even more by having him do my kitchen as well!

This is Ron's recollection of what happened:

At the beginning of my son Ryan's graduation party, Jay came to me and said, "Ron, I need to apologize to you." I said, "For what?" He just smirked and said, "I'm not sure, but I'm sure it will be for something that I don't remember." Just one of the things that he did that night was to steal one of my cordless mics and proceeded to make feedback sounds and other interference noises, knowing that the noises would drive me crazy. Once I found out what it was and who was doing it, I went stomping up the driveway to find him, Gary, and my other son, Bob, giggling. Jay then gave the "Oh-shit" look to me, as he handed me back the mic. Of course, it was impossible to be angry with him for long. Soon, he was cooking up some other plan.

I had to start off this story with a lighter moment from my experiences with Jay, as I am going to attempt to tell the story of my experience with him, his mom and his family during his final two days, and final seconds of life on this earth. For some reason, I was picked to be the one who was blessed…and cursed…with holding and watching a young man die who was, by all accounts, Superman. He cheated death so many times in the past that I, and I suspect all of us, thought that he was just going to do it again. The death sentence that he had been handed had been given to him before and it wouldn't be unlike him to beat it again. We all believed that. After all, would someone who sent the following message be giving in to cancer?

From 315-335-6771
Hey Ron. It's Jay Wilhelm…. Do You Mind if I use you as a reference for a job app?

Received
Apr. 9, 08 12:04 p

Not being one to do a lot of texting, I just phoned him back and said, "Jay, how many freaking Jays do you think I know?" I told him that I would lie and give him a good reference, never believing that 47 days later, he would be gone.

During those 47 days, I was getting the updates that I suspect everyone was getting - and they didn't sound good. I knew of the news from Rochester that they had exhausted their resources and had no other possible course of action. They were sending Jay home. Bob and Jay were close, so Bob was our informant on Jay's condition and gave us updates on a regular basis. He told us that there was a possibility of an experimental treatment in Texas somewhere and that Tammy was going to try to get him in there.

Then came Memorial Day, May 26ᵗʰ, 2008, and the phone call from Tammy. She explained that Jay had asked her to call me to see if I could remodel the bathroom for his Mom. Apparently, he wanted her to have a really nice tub to soak in, with water jets and all. They had picked out a new vanity, sink, lights - just about everything for a new bathroom. She explained that time was a factor - so was keeping the bathroom usable, as Jay wouldn't be able to climb the stairs to the other bathroom because of his weakened condition.

'Are we talking about Jay?', I thought? 'Can't be! He can make it up the damn stairs anytime.'

My wife, Karen, and I were taking the afternoon off when I took the call. We were driving around through car lots and I told her that

I would be over first thing in the morning to look at it. After hanging up, I thought, 'Hell, we are just a couple miles away. Let's go over right now.' So, I called her back and we went right over.

At Bob and Chrissy's wedding reception, Jay and Dan had schemed up an idea to do a take-off on a scene from the movie Old School, where a character talks about a midget coming out of the closet and tag-teaming his girlfriend. So, when it was Jay's turn to give his Best Man speech, Dan grabs the mic and starts into his act. At exactly the perfect moment, Jay stands up, takes the mic away from him, gives a great speech and saves the day. Classic!

Jay was thinner than I had ever seen him. He was in severe respiratory distress and was as pale as a sheet of white paper. I was a field paramedic for quite a few years, so I knew that this wasn't good. But this was Jay! He still greeted us with a smile, hugged Karen and chatted as much as he could. Tammy, as usual, was grateful, gracious, and caring, as she showed me the bathroom.

I asked both Tammy and Jay if they wanted me to wait until he was feeling a little better before we got started. They both said that they would like for it to get done as soon as possible. There was an unspoken sense of urgency, felt by both Karen and me, and as we got in the car to go home we spoke of it. I spoke then of things being grave. But for some reason he wanted this done.

I phoned Bob and told him to round up a

couple of guys, if he could. So, he started making calls. I know he got a hold of Dan, who said that he would be over right after work. Ryan said the same thing. Bob said that he and Chrissy would come down so that when Ryan and Dan got there, we would be ready to start putting things back together.

I went home to pack all of my tools, as they hadn't really been used since we built the store, and made a plan for the next day. Step one was just to gut everything - except the toilet.

May 27, 2008, I woke up a little earlier than normal. My paperwork went unusually smoothly, orders were complete and I was out the door. I phoned Tammy to see if it was too early to come over. She said that it was fine to come and I headed that way. Bob and Chrissy were going to be a couple of hours behind, but they would be there early as well.

Quite a few years ago, Jay was at the house around the Christmas holiday for just a typical visit. On New Years Day, Ryan and I decided to start a project of relocating the stairs that went to their bedrooms. While Karen was visiting her dad, Ryan and I basically gutted the better part of the living room, stairs and upstairs. By the time Jay came back a week or so later, the living room was twice as big, the stairs were in a much nicer location, and the whole upstairs had changed. In the way that only Jay could do, he looked at me and said something like, "Do you just get these funny freakin' thoughts to tear down walls and stairs and shit and then just decide to do it?" He had the gift of being a wise-ass but without offending people. Maybe the stair project was why he chose me to rebuild the bathroom.

I walked in the door and Jay was sitting on the couch with his oxygen mask, looking worse than the day before. I asked him, "How you doing, Jay?" He said that he was fine and then, uncharacteristically, he said, "Actually, I'm not doing too good today. I had a rough night." This isn't good, I thought. Jay was always swelling with optimism. By this time, Tammy was back in the room and I told them both that we didn't have to do this now. It could wait until Jay was feeling better. But they both said to go ahead and start - so that's what I did.

Tammy was sitting with Jay every free moment. She was reading to him, mostly what seemed to be Bible passages. When she went out of sight for more than a few seconds, Jay would call for her, in a somewhat panicked voice. Tammy would come running and sit with him and read some more.

Actually, I was mostly singing to Jason. He had asked me to tell him stories of when he was little. I was so emotional at that point, I could barely think, on the verge of tears, but not wanting him to see that.

I said, "Jay, you know my mind is like a sieve and I can't remember anything on the spot like that!"

So, he said, "Then sing to me."

112

I panicked. How was I going to do that? But, he just said "Strawberry Wine". So, I sang. "Strawberry Wine," "Holding You," and I can't remember what else; but it really seemed to help keep him calm enough to keep his breathing as regular as possible.

I thought about it after and wished I had thought of the time he was about four or five and I took him to The Enchanted Forest with a work group. We walked in, and he wanted to play one of the boardwalk games. I thought, "We'll just get that over with so he doesn't tease all day!" He played the game where you throw the ring over the soda bottles, which I told him was impossible to win. Of course, the first set of rings he tried, he got a ringer! He won a HUGE stuffed Gumby. It was almost as big as he was! He was so excited.

Then, later that day, we were on one of the rides, the Tilt-a-Whirl I think, and I went on with him, forgetting that it had been quite a few years since I had gone on carnival rides. I was so NOT having fun - I thought I was going to be sick. I must have been green, because the kid running the ride slowed it down and said to me, "Ma'am, would your son like to get off now?"

He was so embarrassed and I think that was the first time he ever thought of me as "old." I wish I could have thought of some of the stories in this book, but I am so glad I was able to sing to him that day and comfort him when he needed me to be strong.

I was two days from sending the book to the printer when my mother finally sent me an email. She had been struggling and struggling with the emotions of the situation. I wish I could have thought of all of these that day, too.

Grandma writes:

Tammy, I know this is late but I just can't seem to put my thoughts into words.........there are so many memories .....starting on the day he was born.. all of us piling into Cheri's VW so we wouldn't miss it...Finding babysitters for him every other week...None of them appreciated him!   When he fell at Cheri's pool and broke his tooth. When he was in Christine's wedding with Jennifer...He was so little and thought he was so big! The high school prom when I came to Camden to see them all dressed up (he was so handsome in his tux). It was a rainy night and so cold but they had to come to Rome to the Savoy for dinner....I thought I was so smart getting to the Savoy parking lot to take more pictures. They were freezing but stood there for Grandma to get another picture.. He was always so polite...When he was little and the kids would get into trouble at Grandma Campbell's house, Jason was always the one who got the "time out"...

How happy he was when Erin became his sister...It was one of the biggest things in his life...He loved having a sister.. All the baseball games he loved so much.. When he knocked the ball over the house at the Camden field...so excited because Grandpa saw it...and bragged about it so many times after. When Joey started playing baseball, Jason knew he was going to be so good at it and couldn't wait for his games.........or Tommy playing the drums ....He was so proud of him, and amazed he was so good.

*****

Ron continues:

In the meanwhile, we were working away, quiet as we could, not talking unless we actually had to. An unspoken sense of urgency was all through the room as we uncovered more and more structural problems. Keeping the toilet in place was the main thought. The floor was rotted so badly, though, that we had to replace joists and flooring. The toilet had to come out. Bob ran and got supplies, and Chrissy and I pulled it out, making sure that Jay didn't have to use it first. Bob came back. We fixed the floor under the toilet and put it back in. There was still a large hole into the cellar from where the shower stall was, but at least we got the toilet back in. It was not a minute too soon.

At a little after 1:00pm, Jay needed to use the bathroom. I explained to Tammy that she would have to be really careful with the hole in the floor. She and Jay went in. My very first thought when she told me that he needed to go was not a positive one. It's never a good thing when someone who hasn't been eating or drinking has to go to the bathroom. We sent Bob for more materials and Chrissy and I went outside to sit on the steps. What a beautiful day it was! The sun was shining and it was warm. But I sat there thinking again and again, 'This isn't good. This isn't good.'

Those that know Chrissy know that she doesn't stay still very much. If she can't do anything physically, she usually just chatters away. Well, Chrissy was chatting and chatting to me and all I could think was, 'This isn't good. This isn't good.' Although I remember most of the details of that day, I cannot recall a word that Chrissy was saying. I kept going back inside, listening for Tammy or any noise that would give me a sense of what was going on. Nothing! It seemed like forever. Finally, Bob got back and the three of us were now waiting. A couple more trips inside and still nothing…..

Finally, Tammy came out.

At Bob & Chrissy's rehearsal dinner, we decided that there would be no clanging of glasses to make them kiss. That would be too tacky. If anyone wanted them to kiss, someone, or a group of someone's, would have to stand up and sing a line of a song with the word 'love' in it. The wedding party was full of musicians, so you knew that something special was going to happen the next day.

The singing began…..A person here, a table there, then the bridesmaids, then the groomsmen. It was like a damn Broadway musical! And then we heard it.
Beat Box! It went on and on and then Jay appears from the bar in the front room, carrying the mic, (I think I see a pattern!) beat boxing and dancing his way out in perfect rhythm like he had been planning and rehearsing this for months, finally ending with "Love is, what I got." The place went crazy. Only Jay!

Tammy was crying as she said "Ron, Jay

116

needs you." As we were going in, she said that he wasn't responding well to her. As I opened the curtain to the bathroom, he struggled to lift his head and we made eye contact. He tried to reach for his shorts to cover himself but I told him not to worry. I'd seen it before. We started to walk him out and I asked him where he wanted to go. He couldn't speak; so I asked him if he wanted to go to the couch. He said no. I said, "How about the bedroom?" He nodded yes. By this time, I had yelled for Bob to come in, as Jay was totally dependent on us getting him to where he needed to go. Bob grabbed his feet and I lifted his upper body and we took him into the bedroom. Tammy said that he can't lie down. I told her that I knew and that I would sit with him in the bed. I consciously knew why we were going into the bedroom and at the same time, I had peace with it, with knowing what was going to happen. At some point, Bob took most of his weight and I sat on the bed as Bob set him down. I sat behind him; he leaned back, and took one last breath and that was it. No pain. No drama. Just rest…at last.

Tammy had just stepped out to call her mom to have her come over. When she stepped back in seconds later, Bob and I told her that Jay was gone. She said, "He can't be gone! It's not time. It's not time. There're things he has to do." As Tammy went to call 911, Bob and I moved Jay onto the floor and started CPR.

Just as we started CPR, my cell phone rang. I didn't answer it then, but later retrieved the voicemail from Ryan, saying that he got out of work early and that he was on his way over. The time of the voicemail was 2:16PM.

> *Bob was doing compressions and I was doing mouth to mouth. Bob was a little worried that he was going too deep or not deep enough with his compressions. I just told him to relax….that there was nothing that we could do to hurt Jay now. His apprehension was understandable, as he was watching his best friend die. I just told him that Jay was already in a better place and we couldn't hurt him.*

> *While waiting for the ambulance to arrive, Tammy came back in the room and asked what she could do. I thought that she should probably just leave the room and wait for the ambulance, to avoid seeing what was happening, but Bob did something well beyond his years. He told her to kneel down beside Jay and hold his hands. Tammy did, and then she prayed while Bob and I just counted and kept rhythm. It was a very peaceful moment and I remember thinking that he has the softest lips of anyone that I have ever known. It's no wonder he had so many girlfriends!*

I don't think I asked what I *could* do, but what I *should* do, because I had no idea. I remember crying, "No! I'm not ready!" But after I knelt down by Jason and realized that we were at that point, I remember the feeling of a protective wall going around me. It was very strange, but I knew what was going to be ahead, and I knew I had to help my mother, and father, and Joey, who was in the living room. I remember hearing him scream and start to cry. I didn't know what to do. I wanted to stay with Jay, but I knew that Joey needed me, and my mother had walked in right at that point as well, and I couldn't help Jason anymore. I went out into the living room and hugged Joey and my mother. I remember thinking almost immediately that Jason picked the bedroom because Joey was in the living room, and he wanted to protect him. I am absolutely sure of that, after thinking about it in the weeks after.

Chrissy had called Andy and he was there in less than two minutes.

I called Cheri to tell her.

Cheri:

>*I was at my desk on Tuesday trying to catch up from the previous week when the call came from Tammy. She was crying and she just said, "He's gone."*

>*I must have screamed because the other people in the office came running and Dave wasn't here. The next thing I remember is saying, "What do you mean gone?"..... and Andy getting on the phone and saying, "I don't know how to tell you this, Cheri, but Jason passed away."*

>*I couldn't believe it!! Not now! We weren't ready. He had to be at his party! I think that I just never accepted that he really wasn't going to be at it until that moment.*

>*Then I had to leave, crying all the way home, to tell my kids . Of course, everyone was shocked and crying, but Jennifer collapsed into a sobbing heap on the floor and we all just cried. I know that this was why I left to come home, because I had to be there to tell my kids.*

One of the girls told me that Jason had talked to them and said, "I didn't want your mother to leave - I wasn't done with her yet." If only I had known I obviously never would have left.

My niece, Jennifer, is Cheri and Dave's oldest. She is also the oldest grandchild, and Jason was the second, and they are only eight months apart, so they have always had that connection. It was a good thing Cheri was there for her, because it could have been much worse. I had a lot of support here for us. Jennifer and Cheri's other kids needed her there with them when they heard the news.

Ron:

The ambulance came....so did scores of friends and relatives. I wondered where they all came from. I gave Tammy and Andy a ride to the hospital. Her main concern at that time was who was going to be there when Tommy got home from school. 'Amazing,' I thought. Chrissy promised to stay and wait but I think that Gramma Closinski ended up waiting for him. I then had to make the phone call to Ryan and let him know the news. Jason is gone! For me, the most difficult thing in the world to do is to tell someone that a loved one has passed. I went home, got a glass of wine, got in the Jacuzzi and soaked, telling Karen the sad, tragic and amazing story of what had just happened.

The next morning, I had to go back for a couple of hours just to get a permanent floor down and I asked Tammy how she was and she said, "I

*slept great! We both did." How true that must
have been.*

*The magnitude of Jason's impact on life
and people was not clear to me until the calling
hours and funeral. I watched as hundreds of
people streamed in without wanting to leave. Most
people go to a wake with the simple plan of
making an appearance out of respect and then
quickly leaving, but no one wanted to leave this
one. I thought at the time, 'How did this kid, in
his few short years, touch so many lives in this
way?'*

*The bathroom did finally get finished over
the next couple of weeks. It came out great and I
can only imagine how soothing and peaceful that
first bath was for Tammy. I can only imagine that
she sat there, a glass of wine in hand, and raised
her glass in tribute to one of the most amazing
individuals that I have ever known.*

*During the reconstruction time, I learned
what a remarkable mother that Tammy is and I
tasted what people go through after the death of a
loved one. Tammy remained strong, through every
situation...from the people showing up to get the
oxygen tanks, telling them that their services will
no longer be needed...to the innocent friend that
hasn't heard the news and just happens to call.*

*Someday, I will see Jason again and I will
ask him to tell me why it was that I was blessed to
be there, instead of his hundreds and hundreds of
friends and family. Until then, I will remember
Jay as he was in life, drawing strength from his*

strength, laughter from his off-color jokes, and inspiration from the stories and memories of his remarkable life.

I still believe that the reason Ron was there was because Jason knew he would be able to help me go through that day, and he would know what to do. I can't imagine what I would have done if they were not there to tell me, and help me with him and the whole situation. Again, fate is an amazing phenomenon and it should not be taken for granted.

The people Ron talked about who just magically showed up was mind boggling. My neighbor from across the street came when she saw the ambulances. My brother Jerry and sister in law, Cathy, came from work and again, seemed to be there instantly. Bob Fleming's sister Margaret was there. I hadn't seen her in such a long time, I looked at her coming toward me when we were getting ready to go to the hospital, and I was dumbfounded. How the heck did she know - it had literally been fifteen minutes. The ambulance was just leaving the house for the hospital. It turns out she works in the building on the corner, heard and saw the ambulance, and just knew.

My father got there just as we were leaving. I could barely look at him. Everyone thinks my mother has a hard time with emotions, (ok, she does), but this whole experience took an exhausting toll on my father's emotional state as well. He hugged me and just said, "I don't even know what to say to you."

And, we left for the hospital. When I first went into the bedroom, and Ron and Bob were doing CPR, I remember telling them to stop. I said, "He couldn't breathe

when he was alive - I don't think he will be able to now."
But Ron said they had to keep doing the CPR until the
ambulance came. That was another reason why I think Ron
was there. I think I remember him, or someone, telling me
that if Jason was pronounced dead at the house, we would
have had to wait for the coroner, and they couldn't have
taken him to the hospital; it would have been the morgue.
It would have been a drawn out and awful ordeal if we had
to wait at the house and go through that, and not had the
controlled "Good bye" room at the hospital for everyone to
go.

When we arrived at the hospital, the head nurse
came out into the hall and told me they were "Still working
on him." I told her to stop - again saying he couldn't
breathe, and it would be too hard for him. They set up the
private ER room, and there was a conference room across
the hall. She said we could go in with him for as long as
we needed, and anyone who came could wait in the
conference room instead of the outer waiting room.

And they came. Erin came with Jessica and Kelly
Fleming. I remember Kelly asked if she could pray for
him, and I was glad for that. Bob came, and I was glad he
was there for the boys as well. My mother and Joey, Aunt
Betty, I think my brother Joe and Emily came, but I'm not
sure. My cousin Christine and Tyler - I can't remember
who else, but it seemed like the room just stayed full for
hours while we sat with him, although I don't think it was
much more than an hour. I asked for a blanket for him, and
they brought it, without question. The staff was so touched
by the loss as well, we could feel it.

My brother, Jerry, and his wife, Cathy, had gone to
get Thomas at his lacrosse game. I remember when he got
there, still in full gear, just sobbing. I can't help but think

that I didn't prepare Tom and Joey as well as I should have. I know both Jason and I had been telling them for a couple months how he was getting sicker, just to try to soften the blow if something tragic did happen. But, then again, I really thought we would have more time to worry about that.

I guess I did know over that last weekend that he was getting closer. On Saturday, (May 24th) he was complaining about not being able to breathe, and that he didn't want to go to his party the following Saturday if he would have to be in a wheel chair or on oxygen. I told him that was why we were trying to build up his strength, and we had a whole week to do it. He asked me if I believed that, and I said, "Yes. Why? Don't you?" He didn't answer me.

I found this post on his Facebook page, dated May 25th:

Jay Posted: May 25th
Jay is regaining his strength for the party Saturday!! 8:33a

By Monday, after talking to Ron about the bathroom, and him getting so much worse so quickly, I had decided that we could get the bathroom done, and Jay could take a bath on Friday night, have the party on Saturday, and "go home" on Sunday. Looking back, I am not sure if I consciously thought that ahead of time, or after the fact, during the constant replays in my head.

I had called Michelle Wilhelm, I think, on our way to the hospital, and asked her to call everyone on that side. While we were in the ER, it occurred to me that Irene and Phil (Jason's Nana and Grandad) may want to come down to see him, assuming that Michelle had contacted them prior to that. I called them, and Irene answered. I instantly knew that she had not heard. I didn't know what to say - so I started fishing for information. I asked if Phil was home, and he was not. Now I had to decide what to do. I knew she needed to know, but I didn't want to tell her when she was home alone. She had said that Phil should be home at any moment, so I just told her. I still feel bad that she was all by herself, and I wonder if I should have waited.

I still felt like I had a shield around me, allowing me to function and get through those first few hours and days. I remember when we were in the hospital, I was standing next to him, rubbing his head like I used to do all the time to calm him down, talking away, like he was sleeping or something. Maybe it was shock.

The next few days were absolutely amazing. The people who came over, or called or sent food - it was truly never ending. Someone showed me Jason's MySpace and Facebook pages, and the posts from his friends were heartbreaking, and awe inspiring at the same time. My brothers and sister were all there with their families. My cousins, aunts, uncles, friends all came and stayed with us. The owner of the company I work for is a good friend of the family, and he came with my brother, David, and stayed for the whole week with the family.

My parents went with Andy and me to the funeral home on Wednesday to make the arrangements. I honestly had never thought about what we wanted, and never talked about it with Jason, so I had no idea what to expect. The funeral director, Jamie Harper, helped us tremendously with a personal yet professional guide to what we needed to do. His father and my parents had been friends for years, and I think my dad may have coached him in baseball at one point, and it was good to have someone who knew the family. The only thing I was sure of that I had thought about ahead of time was that my friend (and Tommy's Godfather) Wayne Clemens, would be the pastor and take care of the service. It would be appropriate because Wayne had recently become a pastor, and he used to be a drummer in a rock band. Who would be better to perform the service?

But, Wayne had switched jobs shortly before that, and was unable to change his shift to attend the funeral. Oh. I don't remember even missing a beat. After we left the funeral home, we stopped over at Diane Hollibaugh's house, and she was sitting on the porch talking to Jeff Waterman. I told her of the dilemma with Wayne, and asked her if she would help me. I suggested that she, Debbie Kent, and maybe Patti Kimball could put together something for the service. She immediately agreed and was sure that the others would be happy to do that for us. I asked Jeff if he thought the Camden Fife and Drum Corp could play at the service - actually at the cemetery. He had tears running down his cheeks. He said he didn't know if the corps would be able to do that, emotionally, and that Randy and he definitely would not be able to do it. But, he said maybe they could do something at the wake, and he would let me know. I had total confidence that Diane would take care of everything beautifully; she always did. I never could have imagined the incredible service they would put together for us.

Debbie called me and asked me about the music I wanted. Music is such a big part of our life, and Jason's, it was important to get it right. I told her I wanted the song "I Can Only Imagine", by Mercy Me, and I wanted Gary Johnson to do "Let it Be," if he could. Other than that, they could pick out whatever they felt was appropriate. And they did.

Jason's friends all got together in different groups and mourned together. But, they all also used the internet - Facebook and MySpace - to say goodbye and pay their respect to him. I think it was all part of the process necessary, in the new internet age, for them to mourn someone who was such a big part of their lives. I have to share some of these because they began to help me see through the eyes of others how much his friends and peers respected him, and loved him for who he was.

> *Keegan Bushey wrote at 5:57pm May 27th:*
> *live free. live strong. live forever*

> *Markus Anderson wrote at 6:45pm   May 27th:*
> *A Life spent living, is a life never forgotten.*

> *Erica Lynn Schultz wrote at 7:32pm May 27th:*
> *this is so unreal, I just talked to you a few hours ago. I don't even know what to do. when stuff like this happens you're one of the first people I go to for help. You will be missed so much. Rest peacefully Jay. I love you and I'll see you when I get there ♥*

> *Stephen Mitchell wrote at 10:05pm May 27th:*
> *It appears that God needed a drummer.*

> *Eternal rest grant unto him, O Lord.*
> *And may perpetual light shine upon him.*
> *May the souls of the departed, through the mercy of God, rest in peace.*

(Thanks for the title, Steve)

Dennis Clausen wrote at 11:19pm May 27th:
Hello sir,
*I wasn't as close to you as a lot of people but I will
say this....you were a good dude. The last time I
saw you I got to hug you and crack a few jokes.
We got along good. You got along good with
everyone. That is why everyone loves you. I am
sorry you suffered. You may not have gotten to do
a lot of the things you wanted, but your impact on
everyone will be felt forever. Anyone who got the
chance to talk to you was a better person when the
conversation was done. You will be missed and I
am sad you are gone. We will see you again...so
keep the beer cold. Love you dude.*

Gary Johnson wrote at 12:58am May 28th:
*You were my brother, you were my best friend, you
are going to be with all of us forever. You were
responsible for some of the most amazing
moments of my life,*
*And I owe a million moments of happiness to you.
I'm comforted knowing that V will be there with
you, and that you'll be there with her...*
Rest in peace my friend.

Mandy Fitzgerald wrote at 2:44am May 28th:
*Jason Christopher...here I am at 2:42 in the
morning and I haven't even begun to think about
sleeping yet. You were my best friend, my hero,
and my inspiration. There is nothing I wouldn't
do just to have even 5 more minutes with you. I
don't think you ever understood the impact you
had on my life and on all of our lives. I drank a
High Life for you tonight babe! Aren't you
proud? All I wanted was to be with you on*

Saturday celebrating 5 years. Well, it's officially 5 years today and I couldn't be more proud of you. You fought hard until the very end and I love you more than you could ever know. Rest in peace my sweetheart, I'll see you when I get there. *May Angels Lead You In* My best friend, always and forever. Love, MFBF

Kathy Wright wrote at 7:21am May 28th:
I love you and miss you. Words can't explain. Breathe in some fresh heaven air, play baseball with all of your heart, and beat those drums for us all to hear. I know you will Livestrong in Heaven in the way that you showed us all how it's done on Earth.

Tammy Hewitt wrote at 11:19pm May 28th:
Jay...I'll never forget the "crazy kid" jumping from the trees during the Halloween Party.. You brought life to everything you did......
You will forever be a hero and inspiration. You are a true example of the word courage. I am proud to have had the privilege to know you. My thoughts and prayers are with you today and always.

Amanda Harlander wrote at 11:49am May 28th:
Do you remember the 3 am Im-ing sessions, visiting me at school "I live alone", throwing rocks at my window, the most funniest April Fool's Day jokes ever, the Yankees game, Mangoes, New Years 2000? I have spent some of the most fun and amazing times with you. I will never forget a single moment, a single laugh, a single smile. There are so many things I wanted to say, so much left unsaid, but I think you know. You are the

definition of a hero. You left your mark here Jay.
Be proud of yourself. We are all down here
applauding you! I love you and am always
thinking about you!!

Tommy - MySpace
May 28, 2008 10:55 PM:
Jay,
My best friend, my favorite drummer, my hero, my
idol. My big brother. I love you jay always. 5 of
hell- now you're in heaven watching over all of us.
Rest in peace man. I love you so much.
Tom

Rob Anderson wrote
at 12:24am on May 29th, 2008
you were the man jay. your fight was greater than
we will ever know. I will never be the fighter you
were, but I will always strive to be the man you
were!!

Patrick James (Palm Beach) wrote
at 2:44am on May 29th, 2008
Jay Wilhelm was an incredible person. Jay's life
was the purest example of ambition, dedication,
and passion. His memory should serve all that
knew him with support and strength. Jay had the
strength everyday to stand up to life's greatest
obstacle and channel his emotions into his greatest
love outside of his family and friends; his music.
Although the physical loss of this man's presence
will be felt for our lifetimes, the strength and love
that we can take from Jay Wilhelm will be present
for eternity.

R.I.P. Bud

Katie Ramsden – MySpace:
May 29, 2008 8:34 AM
I love you as Whatever & Everything
You always knew how to bring everyone together!
Now you get to sit up there in a big stuffed chair
with an oversized bowl of ice cream and just watch
everyone marvel over you and the lives you've
touched.
I know you're going to be busy making music with
all the great ones but don't forget about us little
people down here, ok?

Brandon - MySpace
May 29, 2008 11:37 AM:
So much to say about a man that would do
anything for anyone that he could...more of a man
than any could possibly be....if I could only go
back to the days we played ball together and had
no problems or worries and just had fun.....instead
its an ending to a battle that was tearing you apart
day by day. Wasn't the way that I saw or hoped it
to be...you'll always be in my heart and never
forgotten.
Keep a close watch over all of us down here and
rock on up there! You're a great example of a real
American hero to me! love ya Jay

Courtney Bates wrote at 3:43pm May 29th:
I'll never forget the day you walked into Mr.
Fanning's third grade class and you and Chad
become best friends instantaneously. We all
thought you were so cool because you told us all
you had Hulk Hogan's autograph on a napkin.

And you were such a pain in Mr. Fanning's ass that he put your desk right next to his and we would race to see who got their work done first. And there were all those nights in middle school when us village-living kids played hide and seek EVERY night during the summer, and the night it rained and you stayed on Heather's front porch with us while Rick played the guitar. There are so many things I will remember about my childhood that include you. Things may have changed the last 10 plus years, but my memories won't. I guess what I'm most thankful for is us girls running into you that Thursday last summer before Josh and I got married. I got to hug an old friend one last time and see a smile on his face. I pray you are at peace, you deserve it.

Erin Fleming wrote at 7:26pm May 30th
I keep thinking that I see you everywhere I go. I still think that you are going to be home when I go there and that this is all just a bad dream. I guess this just hasn't quite registered even though we put you to rest today. I miss you so much, Gay-gay! I have so many memories with you, and I suppose that only you and I understand most of them. When we wouldn't stop laughing and go to sleep and dad came in the room and said "Heads are gonna roll" and we cracked up even harder and longer, "Ree-haww", "I'm not a (sings) Nurf Bow and Arrow!", "What's with all the rompin' and stompin'?" - "All I wanted was a drink"
The time we went camping and you blew up a package of hotdogs with a CO2 cartridge, driving to Rochester and you getting all worked up calling the police about the guy carrying the trailer on the thruway who almost hit us and everyone else on

the road.
The time you visited me in Oswego and asked if Jake could come- which started this whole thing that's still going on 5 years later.
Thank you for what you told me about that. It means the world to me. You were such a wonderful person and I truly believe God put you here on Earth with a purpose to touch so many lives, and now he has called you back because he needs you. I don't know what I am going to do without you, Jay. But you are always here with me, forever and always. I know you are looking down on us now and that you are happy.
Did you hear Tommy make a fart noise at the service today? Trying to make me laugh...something you would do. I see so much of you in Tommy and Joey. You have left your mark on the world, little brother. What a great life you had.
Love always, your big sister.

And they went on and on. They are still posting notes to him to this day, and I read them all, over and over. I hope they never stop. He had 50+ birthday wishes on December 24th, almost 7 months later.

The wake was on Thursday, May 29th, at Nunn and Harper Funeral Home in Camden. It occurred to me the morning of the calling hours that the suit we had brought for Jason would cover the new Tattoo that he was so proud of showing off. Many of his friends had not seen it (he only had it for 10 days). I called Jamie Harper and asked him if there was any way we could lose the coat, and roll up his sleeve so the tattoo would show. I knew from his ever so slight delay in responding that it would probably not be easy; but he said he would take care of it. And he

133

did. It was prominently displayed for all of his friends and family to see.

There is nothing that could have prepared us for the number of people who came and stayed during the four and a half hours. Of course, our family was there in force. All of the extended family, too. Bob's family, the Wilhelm family, Andy's family were all there. There were forty-seven different flower arrangements! But, the line of people was non stop from 4:00 pm until about 8:30. His friends from high school, from work, from the bands, from Camden, from Utica, from Rome, it seemed everyone he had ever met was there! And the amazing thing was that each one of them had a personal connection to him that was strong and deep and real. He left an imprint of his personality and character on everyone he met, and they all told me they would carry it with them and cherish their memories for the rest of their lives.

I had mentioned to Gary Johnson to ask people to bring their favorite picture of Jason to the wake, to make another collage. They brought so many, we needed two boards. Plus, the Tobiasz' sisters had a collage of their own they made, that I think they had planned on giving him at his party on Saturday. It is beautiful, with drumsticks engraved with "Livestrong" on the top and bottom of it. It hangs in my living room today.

And one of my personal favorites, of Bob and Chrissy Scales' wedding - particularly of her father, and the "lap dance" that Jason and Dan Reidy gave him to "welcome" him to the gang! Chrissy's family came through the line. He was with her mother, and her brother, and I had never met any of them. But, I recognized him immediately from the pictures in the lobby. He took my hand and started to introduce himself and say what a fine, respectable son I had. But, I couldn't help myself. I interrupted him and whispered, "I know who you are. I recognize you from the pictures of the lap dance in the lobby!" Well, he didn't know what to say and turned beet red! Then he looked at me like - "Ah, well, that explains it!" Bob later gave me a video of their wedding that showed the whole dance. They were brutal to that poor man!

But they were so gracious, and had so much respect for him, and the role he played in Bob and Chrissy's life.

One of the best surprises of that night was Aunt Jan and Uncle Bill coming. They had told me on the phone a few days before that they were not able to make it to the funeral. They had planned a trip to my cousin David's house for their grandchild's graduation party on Saturday. I wanted so badly for them to be there for the service. They had helped us out on so many occasions throughout the five years. They didn't know Jason well and I wanted them to have a sense of the person he was, and how much admiration he had gained from his peers and the people who knew him. I have great respect for them both and I wanted them to know that the respect and love they had given to Jason was well placed and well deserved. Plus, they are the head of the Campbell family now that Grandma Campbell is gone, and it didn't seem right not to have them there. I was so relieved when they came across the room during the wake.

I think they were astounded for the two days just talking and listening to and watching the people who knew and loved Jay. My Uncle Bill commented that they have been to dignitary services for very prominent people that could not rival the respect and honor for Jason in that room. That was exactly why I wanted them to be there - to see that admiration everyone had for Jason. Although, I have to say I had no idea it would be so over whelming myself!

Jim Harper (owner of Nunn and Harper Funeral Homes) came into the parlor after we were there a couple hours. He came up to me (skipped the line) and took my hand and said he was sorry. Then he apologized for cutting in line. I said, "It's ok, Jim, it's your house!" I remember thinking that Jamie Harper must have called his father at some point, and I assumed it was to say something like, "Holy *Crap*, Dad, you may want to come out here to see this!"

About half way through the evening, after standing through the unending line of people that was still stretching out the doors, I heard the drums. The Fife and Drum Corps was assembled outside the funeral home and they started playing. I told Andy I wanted to see them and he said, "Just go!" So we went out to the lobby - and so did everyone else.

It was the coolest thing! Jason would have absolutely loved it! The whole place just stood still, while they played perfectly, in full dress, with so much respect for my son you could feel it in the beat of the song they played. I immediately found Jeff Waterman after they were done and told him how much it meant to me and to Jason.

Unfortunately, the line that people had been waiting in for hours was now non-existent. I turned around and saw the unorganized crowd, and yelled, "Well, I hope you all remember where you were in line!" I remember Dave Liddy, (slightly smarter than the average bear) caught me on the way back to the head of the receiving line to give me a hug and extend his sympathies. Good thinking, Dave!

136

We came back to our house and there were a lot of people here. I think all of my siblings, Dave Pennington, my cousins Tom and Ann Campbell, Donald Henderberg, so many people to help us get through. Tomorrow would be even harder.

Andy and I got up very early on Friday, May 30th. Since our bathroom was still torn up, we went to my mother's to shower and get ready. Chris' (Jason's father) family was coming into town, and I wanted to get to the funeral home early to meet them, and give them a chance to show their respect and say goodbye before the service.

Now, if you know my mother and my family, you know that one of our great past times growing up was to see who could make my mother cry over something sappy. She was such an easy target. Actually, even the grandkids would try it occasionally. So, needless to say, this was not something "sappy" and she was, of course, very emotional. So, I had given her something my doctor had given me, and she really held up well through the wake. I told her that morning that I brought her another one for that day, and she said, "I don't think I need it. I did really good yesterday, didn't I?"

We just looked at her. "Uh, yeah, because you took a pill!" That was quite funny, and we all laughed.

We went to Nunn's and met Phil and Michelle Wilhelm and their family. Jason's half sisters, Allyson and Rian, and their mother were also in town; and they came early as well. They told me that Chris was in town, and they weren't sure how he was going to react to the girls being there because he hadn't been speaking to them.

I did call him to make sure there weren't going to

be any problems, but my mother would rather I not relate that conversation………..

There was not an incident, and apparently, Chris used the time that weekend to reconnect with his daughters, and I hope they still have a healthy and happy relationship. I have to say, though, that it is the strangest feeling to talk to him now. After 25 years of constant fear and mistrust and disdain for his lack of responsibility with Jason, now - there is nothing. I no longer have to be wary. I don't have to fear that he will do or say something I will have to amend. He has no control over me anymore. I never again have to worry about Jason's relationship with him. I know some people cannot understand why I am not still furious with him for the (lack of) relationship he had with Jay, but, honestly, I feel free from that anger. I even saw him over the Christmas holiday this year and was able to talk to him and not feel anything - good or bad.

The people kept coming and coming to the service. We knew that the wake was probably one of the largest ever in the area, but did not plan on everyone coming back for the funeral service. I had to keep re-arranging the chairs so that the grand parents, aunts, uncles, and family were taken care of, and they just kept coming. (Yes, strange as it sounds, for some reason, I was the one who was managing the seating arrangements!) At one point, Jamie Harper came to me and said, "Ok, Tammy - I have ONE chair left in the whole building!" He had said afterward to a neighbor that it was probably the biggest funeral they had done in either the Rome or Camden homes. He said they have had some big wakes, but people usually don't attend the funeral unless it's on a weekend, and then not to the extent that came to Jason's.

Little did any of us know that the three women I

138

had trusted to "put together a service" would manage to create the most beautiful, memorable, personal service that I suspect anyone there had ever seen. In hindsight, I truly wish we had videotaped it, as odd as that may sound, because it was so much more than anyone could possibly have expected it to be. Maureen Dourney had the wonderful idea of making booklets for me of the whole service, to give to my family and my children as a keepsake. I am forever indebted to her for that, and I will use that as a reference here to try to recreate the experience.

The Pallbearers were Jason's childhood friends who remained close to him throughout his adult life: Dan Reidy, Randy Waterman, Aaron Wdowin, Chad Hollibaugh, Ryan Cole, and Bob Scales. But, I couldn't overlook the friends he had made that brought him his most recent joy through the music they made. I asked the Blueprint band members to be the "Honorary Pallbearers". Nick Visalli, Sam Famolaro, Steve Anderson, and Kevin Sullivan. Jason loved all of these men and would be proud to have them have such a significant roll in this "Celebration of his Life".

The service began with the song "I Can Only Imagine" by MercyMe being piped through the room, and the lobby- which was filled with people in chairs - and into the parking lot through the open doors necessary to fit all of the people in there.

Then, Patti Kimball opened with a prayer:

We gather here today to give thanks for the life of Jason Wilhelm who shared his life with us. There is much to remember and much to be thankful for as we honor Jason. Each of us gives gifts of ourselves to those we share life with. In his great generosity, Jason gave us the gifts of his love and friendship, and his musical talents. And, although he is gone, they can never be taken from us......

Eternal Spirit, before whom generations rise and pass away, we find that even in the face of death our words can be those of thanksgiving. We are thankful for one who shared his life with us. One for whom love, friends, and family were so important...whose life, despite challenges, was lived with vigor.

For the struggles of his life, and for the triumph of Jason's character over trial, of courage over difficulty, of faith over sorrow, we give thanks.

God grant us such strength in the memory of our son, our friend, our brother that we might be thankful for the gift of life that is given to each of us, and in our hearts may the loss of Jason be balanced by thanksgiving for the life that was shared with us. Amen.

Bless those who mourn, eternal God, with the comfort of your love that they may face each new day with hope and the certainty that nothing can destroy the good that has been given. May the memories become joyful, their days enriched with friendship, and their lives encircled by our love. Amen.

Debbie Kent had called me a couple days earlier. She said if I wanted to write something, she would read it for me. The night of the wake, I showed her what I wrote, and asked her if she could read it for me.

Debbie Kent speaks for Tammy:
It is a privilege for me to have known Jason, to have loved Jason, and to know that Jason loved me. And that I have the special privilege of giving you Tammy's message.

We all know there is a special bond between a mother and a son, and Tammy and Jason exemplified that closeness. Thank you, Tammy, for giving me the privilege of sharing your message.

Tammy's Message:

I want to thank everyone for coming yesterday and today. Even though I am writing this at 6 AM on the morning before the wake, I am guessing between yesterday and today we could have used the stadium and had __ALMOST__ enough room for all the people who were touched by Jason's life, and who touched his life. I can assure you he felt as blessed to be part of your lives as you all feel to have been part of his.

He loved being from Camden. He loved the small town atmosphere, the people, the way everyone rallied around anyone who needed it. He loved it that everybody knew everything about everyone within five minutes.

When Jay was diagnosed five years ago, I remember dragging him to our first relay for life - not having any idea what it was - other than a "cancer thing". I remember that we were both so moved by the whole experience, we ended up just standing in the middle of the field, holding each other and crying. While that moment started the most public chapter in his life, it certainly didn't define who he was. I think the greatest tribute to him is the message sent out from his band to all of their friends. They told everyone how he didn't let his illness dictate what he could and couldn't do. He never used it for an excuse to be less of a person than he was meant to be, and he always tried to be there for the people who depended on him.

I want to speak now to those people who meant the most to Jason - and I won't name names, because you all know who you are - his best friend, his favorite ex-girlfriend, his favorite aunt and uncle, the one in his band he was closest to, his favorite teacher/mentor, the people who he let know were the most special and the dearest to him - I want you all to know he loved each of you with all his heart. But, I have to let you in on a little secret now; everyone in the room right now is thinking I am talking to them. That was Jay's gift to everyone he cared about. He made you feel like you were the most important person in his life. And the truth is, you were!

I would like everyone to know that the party at the lake is still on. I realized early Thursday morning that, once again, even in his passing, Jason was looking out for everyone else. We had talked about having his "5 year" party way back in January. When we went to plan it a few weeks ago, he was still strong, and so looking forward to seeing everyone and saying "good-

bye". But, the last few weeks were very hard on him. I know you all are sad and regret that he couldn't have had just a "few more days" - I said it myself. But, then I realized he decided if he wasn't strong enough to enjoy the party with you physically, he would leave early enough for us all to grieve today, but be able to feel him spiritually at the party as he would have wanted it to be. Laugh, cry, tell stories, play music - and keep him alive in your hearts with a positive energy that will carry you through. And please, keep posting messages on his Facebook and MySpace pages. You can't imagine what a comfort that has been to me.

I just want to specifically thank a couple people. I am a true believer that people come in and out of our lives for a reason. Because of a fate timed phone call the day before, Ron and Bob Scales were with us at home when Jason left us. I will forever be grateful for your generous, unselfish offer to help us that put you right there where we needed you to be when his time came. I know he was calmer knowing you were there with me.

I also want to thank Andy Box and his family for coming into our lives when they did. His strength and calmness, his patience with Tommy and Joey and taking care of them when I had to be away with Jason made my life so much easier. I truly could not have managed anything without his support and love. I believe Jason was finally able to relay that to him when we were at the hospital this last time. My family shares Jay's love and admiration for him as well.

143

Then, she motioned for me to get up to speak. I remember saying something about people saying how strong I was, but that I was getting my strength from Jason-and the little pills that Dr. Kirk gave me. It was a nice cocktail.

> *"Jay:*
> *You were such a trooper. Your strength and courage inspires me. Stay by me and let me draw strength when I need it. I love you and I'll miss you every day.*
>
> > *Mom"*

*****

Steve Quenneville performed "I Wonder What They're Doing in Heaven Today," and Rick Kimball played "Keep Me In Your Heart For a While." Beautiful.

Diane Hollibaugh:

> *Today we celebrate the life of Jason*
> > *With love and fond memories*
> > *With words and music*
> > *With tears and laughter.*
> *A short life that will long be remembered.*
>
> *But, before I start, I have heard so many regrets--*
> *From so many of you over the last few days.*
> > *Regrets that you didn't get home sooner.*
> > *Regrets that you didn't phone more often.*
> > *Regrets that you couldn't have practiced*
> *one last time with Jay.*
> > *Regrets that you couldn't apologize for*
> *some long ago indiscretion.*

Regrets that you didn't tell him how much he meant to you.

Regrets that you couldn't give him one last hug.

Regrets that you didn't have more time with Jay.

We can't continue with those regrets. That is the past, and we can't change the past. Frankly, Jay probably has the best seat in the house, knows exactly how you feel, and would be the first to forgive.
We are here to do exactly what Jason wanted --to come together and celebrate family and friends. And come you did.

From California and Florida
From Arizona and Virginia
From Texas and Colorado
To name just a few.

And celebrate we will-- just as Jay planned.

Tomorrow's party was important to Jay, and we must put our regrets behind us and learn from them.

As many of you know, with this terrible disease called cancer, much of your prognosis and treatment is measured by a five-year landmark. It was so important that he had a rose with the date May 28, 2003, the day of his diagnosis, tattooed below the rose. Technically , our young friends say he made it because this was leap year, and there is one more day to the calendar this year.

I still remember the first time I saw Jason,

grade three. Camden Track and Field Day for Camden Elementary. Chad had told me about this "cool, new kid" in Mr. Fanning's class. Mr. Fanning pointed out the new kid to me and told me what a bright boy he was. Later, when I told Jason what Mr. Fanning had told me, Jason told me that Mr. Fanning was absolutely right, but he tried to hide it.

It seemed as if from that day on, Jason became a part of our family - as he did with many families, and our boys with theirs. That quote-- that it takes a whole village to raise a child--was so true for this group of boys growing up. And there were times when I thought we weren't going to make it through the teenage years, but I was actually in awe last night as all these young men and women came through.

Last night, I laughed as Thomas and Joseph were remembering all the pranks that Jason and the gang played on them. For example, one night when my older daughter was babysitting the boys, Chad and Jason sneaked out on the porch roof and were making these weird noises as if the house was haunted. They were successful, but it was my daughter who was the most frightened, not Thomas and Joseph. The boys were used to Jay and his friends.

Perhaps it was the long Camden winter that made these guys restless, and some of their amusing escapades got them into hot water. The snowball wars, and, only last night did I learn that one night after a heavy snow, they hooked Jason up to a truck and towed him up and down the road

146

on his skis. I must have looked shocked, as they reassured me that it was okay - there was a lot of snow on the road, and it wouldn't hurt the skis. It wasn't the skis that I was worried about.

There are a million stories out there about Jason, and we are going to hear some of those memories in a minute. In a service like this, someone always takes time to praise and talk about a life well lived--whether it is true or not. In Jason's case, you can see by the people who came to pay their last respects how he touched so many lives. Not just with his music, or his struggle with cancer, but in everyday life. Jason was truly interested in those around him. When he came to visit me less than two weeks ago, in fact it was Tammy's birthday, and she was taking a phone call, and he worried that his ordeal was just too hard on her. His concerns were about his brothers, seeing his friends a last time, yet still hoping that he might find just one more experimental treatment that might give him more time with his family and friends.

Jason's recent group, The Blueprint, is so aptly named. Jason laid a blueprint with a strong foundation in his family, and he plumbed and wired his life with great friendships. Jason finished his structure with great acts of kindness and concerns for others - not just as an adult, but he started early in life thinking and doing for others. I will never see a drum that I don't think of Jason, and remembering him trying to teach my youngest son a particular beat. Nate's own two brothers had long given up on him, but Jason kept working along and encouraging Nate. Typical

147

Jason. One of those images that you tuck away forever. Or the time that these boys--all pretty good baseball players--all with their different team's uniforms were trying to help this young kid to swing the bat. You could see the admiration in that little guy's eyes.

Jason was a hero to many, and today we celebrate Jason. Yesterday, when we asked Bob Fleming if he wanted to speak or perform, he said "no", he just wanted to sit and feel all the love in the room. And Bob must be comforted by this love.

And that is how we can continue Jason's legacy. We put away our regrets and show our love for each other. Form bonds, listen to each other. It isn't about possessions, it's about our concern for each other. When Jason passed, there became a void in everyone's life. I can guarantee that there will be days when this void is so large that it will obscure your thinking, and you will question what is important or how you can continue with everyday tasks. That void will always be with us, and while it will grow smaller with time, it should also remind us of the Prophet's words:

In Jason's absence that which you love the most about him is clearer
Just as the mountain is clearest to the climber when he is on the plain.
Let there be no purpose in friendship except the deepening of spirit.
Jason has taught us that we should not seek our friends when we have

Hours to kill, but we should seek them
always with hours to live. Light a
    Candle in Jason's name. Let there be
laughter, and the sharing of memories,
    For it is in the dew of little acts that the
heart finds it's morning and is   *refreshed.*

Jason, we all love you, and I hope you enjoy these
memories.

Then, people got up and talked about their own memories
of Jason.

Michaele Morehouse:

    When I think of Jason, what always comes
to mind was his giving nature. He was always
there to help. I remember many Wednesdays in
the spring when Jason would help out with the
Middle School Marching Band percussion line.
Or the time he got an emergency phone call to fill
in for the Middle School Jazz Ensemble. It was
the day of the spaghetti A-pass dinner. The
Middle School Jazz Ensemble was to perform;
unfortunately, the drummer got in a little trouble
and couldn't be at the dinner. Jason was there
that night performing with the "little" Middle
School students.

    Even on this, the saddest of days, I cannot
think about Jason without smiling because of his
wonderful sense of humor. The High School
Band went to competition in Boston. A piece of
tape was placed on all of the students' doors after
lights out. Jason kept slipping notes to us under
the door and signed them "Mr. X". When it was

149

*time to come home, the back seat of the bus was
taped off and reserved for "Mr. X."*

*I feel so lucky, fortunate, and blessed to
have had such a talented, giving, and caring
young man in my life. The Music Department will
truly miss your encouragement and knowledge.
I'll miss you, 'Mr. X!'*

Aunt Mo - Maureen Dourney:

*One summer Jason and Chad decided
they'd become millionaires. Their business was
making hemp bracelets, necklaces, and key rings.
They worked very hard making them and putting
in various stones, gems, etc. Of course, Chad's
mom and gullible Aunt Mo were the "cash"
behind the needed supplies.*

*They began selling in front of Chad's
home. Later it was suggested to them to sign up
for various craft fairs in the area. They did a
small one in Rome, but they were very
disappointed that they did not sell many items, nor
did they make much profit from their day at the
fair.*

*Next, Aunt Mo suggested they get a booth
at a fair that was going to be held in the park in
Herkimer (her hometown). They drove Tom's
truck down and set up shop. It was a hot humid
summer day. Aunt Mo's sister, Judy, lived in
Herkimer and went to see what they had to offer
and to provide them some income. The crowd was
smaller than expected. Bored, Chad crawled in
the back of the truck and proceeded to fall asleep.
When Judy arrived, she spoke with Jason and*

looked over their products and purchased a bracelet to give to her goddaughter. Chad, however, had no clue she'd been there as he slept through the entire ordeal.

One of Jason's best friends from grade school up was Kathy Wright. She had remained a constant in his life and I know he loved her very much. She wrote this and was able to stand up and read it to everyone that day. Such strength, I could actually feel it coming from her.

Kathy Wright:

They say it's better to have one best friend rather than 100 acquaintances. But Jay had 100 best friends - it was just the type of person he was. He was the best friend we all could lean on, learn from, and laugh with because of the type of person he was. There were so many different amazing parts to his personality:

There was the Musician part of him, which is what he was mostly made of:
Stone Soup, Yellow5, IDMA, 12:24, Post No Bills, 60 Cycle Hum, The Morning After, and his biggest love and the center of his life Coersion which became The Blueprint.

Most conversations I ever had with Jay included something about one of these bands. Music was what kept his soul so beautiful. I remember him getting home from spending a week hooked up to chemotherapy and playing his heart out that same night in a show. He was always so proud of his band and their accomplishments.

151

*He was also always the friend you could
count on to make you laugh:*
*I remember the days of being in band in high
school. One day he decided it should be Hum Day.
Hum Day consisted of him giving a cue, and
everyone had to start humming. In the middle of
the period, there was a room full of humming
people, and as you can guess quite difficult to
figure out where it was coming from. Another
day, he made everyone tip over their music at the
same time on cue. He was the one who got
everyone to switch instruments the day there was a
substitute. Jay was the one who rode his
brother's scooter through the hallways of the high
school. When Napoleon Dynamite came out on
video, he was the one who made me sit through it
because "it is the funniest movie ever!" Jay,
Joann, Gary, and I once took a weekend trip to
New York City and his bright face and personality
made it the weekend of a lifetime. And Jay is the
one who shared so many inside jokes with each of
us- ready and willing to reminisce about them at
any time."*

He was a shoulder to lean on:
*We all know that the past five years have
just been a rollercoaster ride of fighting and being
strong for Jay. But no matter what he was going
through, he was a shoulder for each of us to lean
on. He was familiar with getting phone calls at
any time of day when I was in tears or just
outraged about something. My problems were so
trivial compared to his. But he was the one I
could count on to make me strong. When he told
me I could be strong, I believed I could do it- I just
looked at him and knew that if he could, we all*

152

can. He was a rock through all of this, yet was still always there for us.

He was the strong one who took every obstacle in stride, kept looking forward, and kept his head afloat:
When bad news came, he always just kept moving forward. He was a fighter who knew how to live strong. I remember the day he was diagnosed. That night we went out to the Snubbing Post in Rome and he played drums at Open Mic Night- he wasn't the type to sit home and dwell on the bad.

"One year he spent New Year's Eve tied down to his bed by chemotherapy. New Year's morning, Gary, Joann, and I walked into his room equipped with noise makers, party hats, and sparkling grape juice. There he was with a smile on his face, just happy to be with friends, not dwelling on the bad.
He once told me that he was glad it was him who was sick, and not any of his other friends. He told me he knew he was strong enough to handle it. He has a family who has been so strong through everything. A mother who loves him so much. I remember how much he loved to hear her sing; especially at the Relay for Life- that is what he looked forward to. This is part of why he was so strong.

When he would be in Rochester tied down by chemotherapy for a week, he would be the one to be up and walking around the hospital, determined to stay strong. When he was bald, he wore it with style and made the best of it. After his

153

surgery, he had the biggest scar and embraced it and called himself Scar Belly.

He showed us all that life is too short to feel sorry for ourselves. Jay taught us all that giving up is not an option- we need to keep our heads up, move forward, and not look back. He taught us all how to Livestrong. He was a best friend to so many, a jokester, a shoulder to lean on, and a rock for so many of us. This is what we will always remember about him.

Molly Kimball:

Jay and I butted heads pretty frequently-- usually about the most trivial stuff. He was stubborn and had his unwavering inability to be wrong--and coming from me, that's saying something!

But we found common ground in a mutual love for being argumentative and a mutual disdain for stupidity. And our disagreements were always backed by a sincere friendship and understanding.

Jay, you delighted in never letting me win, and you made sure not to mask your delight, either. But you always made me laugh, especially when I was trying my hardest to be really mad at you.

You challenged me more than anyone else I've ever met, whether it was in a good debate or an existential investigation or the occasional game of on-line dictionary.

I'm grateful for the many memories I have

of you, and the few particularly significant ones. I know I'll see you again. Thank you for touching my heart in a way that only you could.

There were more memories that his friends shared that, unfortunately, I don't have copies of; but I asked Aaron Wdowin to send me the story he shared about his trip home for Jason's 5 year party.

Aaron Wdowin:

"Jason says Goodbye"

As the plane landed I turned on my cell; I had several missed calls and a txt from Ryan Cole telling me "we need to talk". I called him as I was walking out of the plane and he told me that Jay had passed. I felt heavy and my pace started to slow as I walked towards the gate that would take me to Syracuse.

As I sat my bags down and said goodbye to Ryan I couldn't stop crying. I cried and cried and cried in front of hundreds of airline passengers who were waiting for flights. I was crying because I felt like I never got to tell Jay how much he meant to me and that now I would never get to say goodbye. I felt like I had abandoned him by moving to California and not being around to help him during his fight.

My fit lasted for about 45 minutes and just as I regained my composer a kid about my age walked by in a Syracuse lacrosse shirt and sat down a few seats away from me. Syracuse had just won the NCAA Championship that day so I congratulated him and asked if he played. He told me no but that he was the strength trainer for the team. As we talked I realized how much he looked and sounded like Jason. He was flying back to SU from Orange County, California, where his mother lived, to be with his dad and girlfriend. I told him I grew up in upstate N.Y. but had been living in Huntington Beach, California for a couple years. He asked why I was heading back home…

We sat and talked for the next couple hours. Originally the layover was supposed to be 45-60 minutes. It ended up being over 3 hours long after several delays. Normally this would have been a huge pain, but because of the layover I got to know Jason - I mean John; it was eerie how similar they were. Both loved to drum and were in bands; as John talked I heard Jason's voice because his was so similar. Both laughed at my jokes and thought I was pretty damn funny; when John laughed I heard Jason laughing. Jason was always quick to laugh and loved to hear my stories about antics at college including football parties, hazing and girls. When I finally told John about Jason and how he passed before I got to say goodbye, he was so empathic and as I teared up he patted me on the back and I swear Jason was there…

I had never met John before that day but we both felt like we had known each other for years. I can't explain it, other than to say that Jason was taking care of me and making sure I knew that he already knew everything I wanted to tell him. I am still in touch with John and plan to be for a long time because even though we all lost Jason so early, I get to see him whenever John and I hang out. John helps me keep his memory alive and I hope to never stop missing Jason or appreciating everything his fight taught me.

I cried as I told this story at your funeral and my tears are falling on my keyboard as I tell the story now. I still miss you so much, Bro. I will never forget the celebration we had at the park that day and I know that you were watching with a smile on your face.

And Tammy, I hope it helps you to know how much we all loved your son. Jason brought our entire community together, reunited old friends, and introduced us to new ones.

JAYCW - Aaron Wdowin

Dan Reidy couldn't speak at the service. He was devastated by the loss, and just couldn't possibly put into words what he wanted to say about Jay. I did finally get him to write down his thoughts, and it was well worth the wait. I believe it belongs here in the timeline.

Dan Reidy:

Who was Jason Christopher Wilhelm? What was it about him that made the people around him love him so dearly? Was it the fact that he was so hilarious and fun to be around or maybe it was his spontaneity? Could it have been the fact that he was so trust worthy and dependable? I am sure that it is all these things and more however I am afraid that my pen lacks the elegance required to

157

describe such a bright personality such as Jason's. However I can tell you what he was to me. Jay was my best friend, a trusted ally, someone who challenged me. He was my "Go to guy", he was also a smartass that wouldn't let me get away with shit; to put it simply; he was the brother I never had. Jay was a guy I could really talk to and count on to give me heart felt advice whether I wanted to hear it or not.

To this day I am resentful for what happened to him and would do any thing to change the out come. With that said I think that people like Jay are chosen for these ailments for a reason. It gives them a chance to demonstrate true strength and redefine the word courage. Only a man as strong as Jay could have endured what he did and at the same time provided a source of strength for those around him. He was the strongest individual I have every met. I consider myself lucky for having known him and am certainly a better man for it.

I miss you brother.

After the memories, Patti Kimball spoke again.

Many of you who know me, know that I like to read the book <u>Tuesdays with Morrie</u> to my classes. It is a story of courage and triumph in the face of death, much like Jason's own narrative.

Morrie has many words of wisdom, some of which I think aptly apply to Jason and how he conducted his own life with grace and determination.

Morrie maintains that there are three keys to finding meaning in life. He says #1 - devote yourself to loving relationships. Looking at all of you today, I would say that Jason did just that; he had many lasting, loving relationships with all of you.

The second key is to devote yourself to your community. Jason certainly did that from helping the Middle School Marching Band, to teaching a youngster how to his a baseball and significantly to his total commitment to the Relay for Life. He devoted himself in any number of ways to his community.

Finally, Morrie advocates that we each devote ourselves to creating something that gives us purpose and meaning. Not only did Jason create in his music, but he helped others create as well...as a band member, a fellow musician, as a sound guy, or as a party planner creating good times for his friends at Festivus.

I am sure Jason never conceived of himself as a role model, but he did truly find meaning and purpose in his life. We would do well to follow his example.

Then she read Walt Whitman's *Leaves of Grass*. Everything was so perfectly coordinated, it was almost like a movie.

At the end, Gary Johnson got up and performed "Let It Be" by the Beatles. I had asked him earlier if he was going to be able to do it, and he said he thought he could. He started playing and was doing so well. Then he got to the second verse, the one Jason had sent him, and started to falter.

We were right up front, of course, and I just kept watching him. When the tears started, I thought, "Ok, he needs help." So, I had to decide quickly if it would be appropriate for me to start singing with him to help him. I waited to see if anyone else was going to do it, and when they didn't, I started singing. Then, one by one, everyone in the place started singing. We all finished the song with him, and it was the most poignant moment of the day.

When the service at Nunn's was finished, we got ready to go to the cemetery. The cemetery was about 10-15 miles away. Jamie stood up and told everyone that we would meet at the Grape and Grog restaurant after the internment. Everyone got up and started the process of leaving. We assumed they were going to the Grog. The cars were filled and Jason was brought out by his friends.

There was a construction crew that happened to be working right in front of the funeral home on the main road. Someone had talked to one of the guys earlier on, and told them that there could be quite a few people coming that day, and they should be prepared for it. When we started to leave, the workers stopped the traffic so the procession could go forward uninterrupted. One of them took off his hard hat and held it over his heart through the whole line. When he saw all the cars lined up, he asked someone if the mayor of Camden had passed away! Some people said that the line of cars stretched over three miles.

They all came to the cemetery. And just as they had done earlier, Diane, Debbie, and Patti had planned a few simple prayers and closure to the wonderful service. When it was over, Rick Kimball stepped up and suggested we end with another chorus of "Let It Be."

Jamie Harper came up to me afterward and asked if I wanted a flower from the arrangement we had brought. I remember he had tears in his eyes. I joked with my father afterward - "Dad, we must be really good to make the funeral director cry!" That just showed me that it wasn't my imagination, but we had just witnessed the most beautiful funeral service ever.

While everyone went to the Grape and Grog, we went home first to change. Then we stopped at the funeral home to get the flower arrangements either to keep or give to the family, and to get the picture boards to bring to the Grog, and the party on Saturday. I understand there was quite a crowd there. By the time we got there, it had started to thin out a bit.

We went home and of course, we had a house full of people. The next day was the party at the lake. I was sure that most of the people would be there, despite the weather forecast of rain most of the day.

The one thing I remember most about that night was that Andy and his sister, Jennifer, worked for a few hours in the garage. I didn't know what they were working on until Andy came in and told me to come out and see. They had taken a picture of Jason sitting at his drums, and blown it up to almost life size and put it on the front of the speaker. They had another picture for the other speaker - it was so awesome! We were using the speakers at the party the next day, and the picture of him playing his drums up by the stage was priceless. He was in so many of the pictures people took that day, either intentionally, or in the background.

When Saturday came, Andy and his father were up and out pretty early. It was rainy, so they wanted to get things set up at the lake before everything got too wet. They took care of everything – even to bringing out a carpet to put the bands on so no one would get zapped. They set up the PA so it was protected from the weather. We brought the endless food up, and Diane Hollibaugh (once again) was there to keep that organized.

When we arrived at the gatehouse at the lake, I remember telling the girl that we had reserved the pavilion three weeks earlier for a party, but that Jason had passed away that Tuesday, so it was going to be more of a memorial party. She told me that the other pavilion near the big one was not reserved, and we could use that if we needed it. It worked out perfectly because we put the food in one, and used the other one for the bands and to hang out.

The weather was so strange. It was rainy everywhere but at the two pavilions where we were. There were storm clouds all around us, but there was blue sky above us, with light, puffy clouds. The sun was shining most of the day on the party. It was lightly raining at the baseball field where some of the people were playing games, which was about 50 yards from the pavilion. You could walk out to the beach, and it was raining there, but we have pictures of two rainbows that were directly over the party. It was amazing. Jason's Aunt Danica has twins who were about four years old I think at the time of the party. Danica told me that her daughter, Tess, (who reminds me of the definition of an "old soul") had told her that she heard Jason talking to God that morning. She said Jason asked God if he could make it not rain on his party, because he didn't think all of his friends and family would bring their umbrellas! I swear, it must have been true, because that is what happened!

And, everyone came! All of my brothers and my sister, their spouses and children, Jason's friends, my friends, everyone Jay would have wanted to be there was there. His aunts, uncles, and cousins on his father's side were there. His father went up to the lake early in the morning, but decided not to stay when people started showing up. That was probably for the best.

There was music all day. Gary Johnson played, Bob's band, Mossback, played. Rick Kimball and Emmett Van Slyke were there and played.   Andy sat in with everyone and played the piano all day long. I got up and did a couple of songs, and my sister and my nieces got up with me. We really had a great time. I sang the songs I sang for Jason that last day. It was hard, but there was definitely a force holding it together. I sang "Somewhere Over the Rainbow" for him, and managed not to butcher it too badly.

Then, the highlight of the day was when the Blueprint got up and played - with Thomas behind the drums. I could tell he had the same electric adrenaline that I was feeling when I was singing. He was awesome, playing the songs exactly like Jason had done, and the band broke down after the set.   It was some pretty powerful stuff.

Later in the afternoon, I got up again, and sang "Bring on the Rain" by Jodee Messina. I remember shortly after Jason was diagnosed, I was playing out with my group, The Boxed Set, when Lisa Murphy and Emmett Van Slyke were playing with us. We were in the middle of the first set, and I called "Bring on the Rain" without thinking

163

about it. I broke down at the first chorus, and couldn't finish the song - I had to leave the stage.

After that, it became somewhat of an anthem. I would sing it to try to strengthen my spirit. I would sing it when I needed to believe that we were beating the beast. I sang it at the benefit that first October back in 2003. It was my "CHARGE" song.

So, I wanted to sing it at the party. And I did, and except for a few breaks, pretty much nailed it. The place went nuts! I noticed that Larry Fox was getting ready to get up and play. JOKINGLY, I called out to him - "Ok, Larry Fox, top that!" It was pretty funny.

I left the stage and was walking toward the rest room. I saw my brother, Jerry, coming back toward the pavilion, crying openly. He was having such a hard time, as were all of my brothers. He met me in the pathway and we hugged. I asked him if he was ok, and he said, "Yeah. That song was awesome, Tam! But, that's not why I'm crying. I'm crying because that poor son of a bitch, Larry Fox, had to get up and sing after that! I would just quit if I were him - and he's GOOD! It's too bad!"
So, we stayed and partied, and laughed, and sang and played just exactly as Jason would have wanted us to. The kids were playing flip cup, and my friend Michelle Morgan and I got in the middle of it and kept right up with them!   We stayed until dark, when the park closed. There were no incidents, everyone pitched in to clean up, and some of the kids came back to our house afterwards. We lit a fire in the back yard, and hung out until about midnight, I think.

Then, after everyone left, my brother Jerry and his friend, Bobby Campanaro, and Dave Pennington were going to the Casino. It must have been about 1am by then. I decided I should go with them. I wasn't ready to sleep yet, and though I never go to the Casino, for some reason, I thought I should go. I grabbed $40, (all I was willing to lose) and went with them.

When we got there, they all hit the ATM and I think took out a couple hundred dollars each. Dave handed me a $100 and told me to play with it. I told him I had my own money, but he insisted. I had never played any of the table games there before. The most I had ever done was play bingo and the slots a few times. At first, I was watching Jerry play at the craps table. I was still pretty tipsy, and could not for the life of me figure out what the hell the object to that was. I saw Pennington over at a blackjack table.

I at least knew the object of the game blackjack, so I went over there to see if I could sit in on that. Of course, it was a $25 table, but I don't think I even realized that until later. I watched a few hands and asked if I could play. Dave was trying to tell me how to do the hand signals at the table. I was trying to joke around with the dealer, and he was very patient with me. So, I started playing, and I was winning, though I didn't realize it at first. After about 15 minutes, Dave picked up the chips in front of me and counted them. He said, "OK, you have $500 here. Put this in your pocket, and use it to finish your bathroom!" (Remember, my bathroom was still torn completely apart and unusable.)

I looked at him and said, "Well, actually I have all the stuff I need right now for my bathroom, but I REALLY need to work on my kitchen!" He just looked at me like he couldn't believe I wasn't excited about winning the $500. Then, he just said, "OK", and we kept playing. About 10 minutes later, he picked up my chips again and said, "Now you have $500 here, and the $500 from before. Is $1000 enough to get your kitchen started?" I said it probably was, and we left the table.

We were looking for Jerry and Bobby. Dave spotted them first. He looked at my brother and said, "Ok, when your brother looks like that, we try not to talk to him too much. He definitely will not be in as good a mood as he was coming out here." And he wasn't. Neither of them could believe I had won $1000 in less than half an hour. I think I almost expected to win. Maybe not that much, but I wasn't as surprised as everyone else was. I wonder if the people monitoring the table saw the little angel on my shoulder helping me out!

*****

A week or two after the service we put a thank you note in the paper for everyone who had been there for us:

APPARENTLY, GOD NEEDED A DRUMMER........

THE FAMILY OF JASON WILHELM would like to extend our sincere appreciation to everyone who shared themselves with us in any way, during our time of great loss. The number of people he influenced in his short 25 years was staggering, to say the least.

The flower arrangements were too numerous to count, and each one was more beautiful than the next. The food sent to our family was enough to feed an army, luckily, because an army of supporters attended his funeral, and the celebration of his life at Lake Delta on Saturday. Please know he loved each of you and was blessed to have you in his life.

We would like to send special thanks to Ron Scales for still being here. Diane Hollibaugh, Patty Kimball, and Debbie Kent for their genuine love and respect for Jason that enabled them to put together the most personal service we have ever seen. And Nunn and Harper Funeral Home, specifically Jamie Harper, for making the most difficult time in our life as easy as possible.

When the storms rage from this day forward, there will be a little more rhythm in the thunder because our drummer is in heaven now, rockin' out!

The posts from his friends on the networking pages kept coming, and I kept up with them whenever I could. Then, when I started asking for stuff for the book, they really helped a lot. Katie Ramsden was always referred to by Jason as "my best friend." He even said she would probably end up being his wife some day. This is what she sent me - though I know it was so hard for her to try to capture the depth of their relationship in a story or two.

My best memory of you? For some reason my mind draws a blank, even though I know there are millions of memories to choose from. All I can think about are those late night drives we took in high school to talk about whatever high school drama we were going through at the time. We would drive around for hours until we had nothing left to talk about and then we'd still sit in

167

the car, sometimes in silence...though deep in thought. Your mom must have wondered why it took half a tank of gas just to get to my house. I still get in my car and go for those drives, but it's not the same without you telling me how ridiculous my troubles are and insisting that I listen to yours now. Other drivers must think I'm crazy when they see me talking to myself, but I know you're there listening and wishing you could chime in with your great wisdom.

Also, this book would not be complete without mentioning Ryan Harlander's porch. That is, after all, where we became friends and where so many of our memories lie. I still get a little nostalgic when I drive by their house. Remember the night that you and Ryan refused to let me get off the porch until I told you something no one else knew about me? I spent a lot of time on the porch that night, but we were best friends by the time you finally let me go home.

...And that was shortly followed with the night we almost drove into the pond. Don't worry Tammy, it's not as bad as it sounds. Ryan, Jay, and I were driving down Dutch Hill Road, going about 20 m.p.h. because Ryan and Jay were in deep mourning over some girls. I was in the backseat wondering why I was riding around with two boys who were so upset over girls. So we're just putting along, all deep in our own thoughts, when out of nowhere I fly up in the front seat with them and we're staring into this pond. Confused about why this pond was in the middle of the road we looked around and realized the road had turned but we kept driving straight... Straight into

someone's lawn and almost for a swim in their pond. We vowed never to talk about that night - I think the guys were a little embarrassed that they almost crashed into a pond at a whopping 20 m.p.h..

Katie Ramsden
(your Katie-girl)

Katie was pregnant when Jason passed away, and she and Nate Skinner had a beautiful baby girl in September. She named the baby Kaela Jaylin, after Jay (and Cailin O'Hara, I think!) I asked her if I could mention that in the book, and she not only said I could, but sent me another part to her Jason story.

> *You can absolutely mention Kaela Jaylin. I don't know if I ever told you the whole story behind it. A couple years ago, Jason and I were watching a show or something where two friends made a pact to get married if they weren't married by a certain age. So I asked Jay if he would make a pact with me that if I didn't have a baby by the time I was 30, I wanted to have a baby with him. Then he said that he was pretty sure he wouldn't be able to have kids, and I promised my first child would have the middle name Jay.*

> *Also, I found an old box in my parents basement the other night and decided to see what crazy things were in it. I found my photography binder with pictures in it of when Jay and I had taken Joe and Tom to Ft. Stanwix. It was years ago; the boys were pretty little. I had completely forgotten it, but it was one of those perfect days. I remember when we parked the car we both looked*

at each other and said, "Want to pretend they're our kids, for the day?

Mike Baker wrote:

     So my senior year of High School I was dating a girl who was at college in Potsdam. One weekend I went up to see her on a Friday after school, planning on staying the weekend. Saturday morning I got a call from my mom, yelling and screaming that I had left without mowing the lawn, which I was apparently supposed to have done days before. She tells me that the lawn has to be mowed that day or else I would be grounded and wouldn't be able to see my girlfriend for weeks. I really don't want to come back, so I called my next door neighbor at the time (on Elm Street), Jay Wilhelm. I ask Jay if he can mow my lawn for me, and without hesitation he said "sure thing." I'm able to stay up in Potsdam the rest of the weekend without my mom killing me.

     A couple of days later I'm over at Jay's house and kind of in passing I said "Hey Jay, thanks for mowing my lawn on Saturday." Tammy overheard me say that, and starts screaming "YOU MOWED HIS LAWN? I'VE BEEN TELLING YOU TO MOW OURS FOR 2 WEEKS!!"
Jay was always willing to do anything for a friend in need.

Amanda Harlander wrote:

     I have SO many memories of Jay like I'm

sure everyone does, but this is not so much a
but something I will always remember him fo

*When I first met Jay I was 17. I remember
telling him that I've always wanted someone to
throw little rocks at my window and wake me up,
(you know how you always see it in movies and it's
just romantic). Well, little did I know that for the
next 7+ years, I would wake up to Jason throwing
rocks at my window and waking me up at 2 or 3
am. This was easy for him because we were
neighbors for a while, but whenever he was in
Camden he would do this. I would get out of bed
and we would talk outside for hours. It always
made me smile and feel good inside because Jay
would remember this. I believe he even did it a
couple times when I didn't live home anymore!!
HAHA!*

*Another thing I'll always have with me was
all the fun we had during my senior year of high
school. We had a group of people we would hang
out with, and we would have SO much fun! We
were having a girls' night one night at Chrissy
Thauvettes house. It was late and we looked out
her bedroom window and who's standing on the
lawn?? Well Jay and Aaron Wdowin of course.
Somehow they got inside and were in Chrissy's
bedroom, then all of a sudden her crazy stepfather knocked on her bedroom door. Jay and
Aaron immediately hit the floor and hid. Her step-
dad says, "Sounds like there's boys in here!" We
all said, "No, it's just the TV." After he left, the
boys got up and just hung out for a bit...I don't
remember how they left without being seen
though-we all got a good laugh out of that one.*

Every weekend we would all get together and have such a blast; going to someone's house, going to Denny's or just driving around and trying to stay out of trouble. Was one of the best years of my life, and I have Jay to thank for that!

I thought this next one was yet another example of Jason putting other people ahead of himself, and always being there to help whenever he could.

It is from:
Sr A Erin Elaine Miller
United States Air Force
San Antonio, Texas
Class of 2002, Camden New York

I am not sure I have a great story to tell but I have known Jay for a long time. I may not have been one of his closest friends, but I knew we were always friends. Any time I saw him out and about there was always a hug exchange and a great conversation to follow. He was one of those people that gave you courage and hope and made you look at life in a new light.

When my mom was dying of cancer, we had a benefit as well. Jay was there. He was a big help and I will never forget the young man that helped to make my mom's benefit a success.

I have been in the Air Force now for three years. I was not able to see Jay before he died or attend his funeral. It hurt to hear what had happened to such a wonderful person, but I felt that pain before when my mom died. Now I know my mother has someone to look after up there.

She will look out for Jay and Jay will be there for her like he was when she needed a good friend. I am sad that he is gone, but I know he is in good hands, and I know my mom now has a good old Camden friend with her. We will never forget Jay and the inspiration he had on our lives.

Aaron Velardi:

The Days of Immortal Youth (or infamy if you were on the receiving end)
Jay and I have had many outrageous and crazy fun filled times. It's so hard to narrow it down to just one. We have done it all, from driving all over the state just because we had nothing better to do that day, to buying fully automatic bee bee guns just to cause whatever kind of havoc we had in our minds that was justifiable at the time.

I remember one time during our last summer together we were on Varick St. and there were a bunch of protesters with their picket signs telling everyone they were going to go to hell for defying the lord and being gluttonous sinning pigs (drinking). Now if you know anything about Jay and myself it's that we liked to indulge in the good old past time of excessive intake of MILLER HIGH LIFE and JACK DANIELS. So what we did was stand on the corner across the street from the protesters and invited them to come and party with us.

Now it's not like we sat there for ten minutes and then walked away. We spent the whole night on that one slab of concrete. We went four consecutive hours of bottles being turned upside down till drained and shot glass after shot glass being filled and taken out like stand still targets. (What I would give to have ten minutes even ten seconds of that night back just to see his face one more time.)

There were many nights like this with Jay that I will cherish till the day I am gone. I will tell my children what an awesome human being he was. How he wasn't scared of anything, because he faced the ultimate unknown more than once. How he was the closest thing to a super hero anyone will ever come to know. Jay was and still is the bravest person I have met in my life. Jason Christopher Wilhelm was more than just my friend; he was my brother, my jam partner, my opposing force of personality, my wingman, and my partner in crime. Hardly a day goes by where I don't look to my wrist and ask him for some kind of assistance to get through my day. I always try and tell myself no matter the pain I personally have endured, nothing can compare to the pain he had felt during his time. He was a true life Superman; he had more strength in his skinny, bony body than most body builders work their entire lives to achieve.

It sucks because I will scroll through the contacts in my phone when I'm looking for something to do, and I will always pass by his name, looking me right in the face, and all I want to do is call him and tell him everything that has happened since we last saw each other. The places I've been, and the things I have seen just play catch up real quick. I will never forget the day it

174

happened. I was feeling really bad because we hadn't spoken in a few months, and I sent him a text message that said "I love you dude" and he sent one back that said "I love you too". It was only a matter of hours later that he had passed-no more than three. I couldn't believe what I was hearing when Colenzo told me the news. It was like someone reached into my chest and ripped the very breath from me.

It still hasn't set in fully yet. I still want to call him and say "what's up? Let's get a beer." But that chance will never come again. What I hope everyone will take from this is to never take anyone or anything for granted. Be peaceful and always remember he is watching you.

And it wasn't just me who thought we had exceptionally rhythmic thunderstorms that first summer. After the first couple of months, I found myself actually apologizing to people for the weather, saying, "I'm really sorry about all the rain, but it's the only time he gets to play his drums up there!" Apparently, everyone was hearing the same thing.

Adam Nolan wrote at 2:42am June 6th
so it's almost 3am and I have class at eight tomorrow and I should definitely be in bed...but instead I'm sitting by my window listening to you bangin' those drums in heaven, and man it sounds great...keep on rockin, love ya bro

Kathy Wright - wrote on MySpace
Jun 6, 2008 4:11 PM
There was a huge thunder and lightening storm

175

last night that I'm sure woke up EVERYONE in Central New York.. It was sooo loud- one of the teachers at my school today was saying how odd sounding the thunder was - almost like it wasn't even thunder. As soon as I heard it, I thought you must have been playing the drums - you played them loud enough and long enough!! I think about you constantly... take care of us! Love you.

Melissa Tobiasz wrote at 10:54am June 7

*God saw you were getting tired, and a cure was not to be, so he put his arms around you and whispered "come to me".
With tearful eyes we watched you, and saw you pass away. Although we loved you dearly, we could not make you stay.
A golden heart stopped beating, hard working hands at rest. God broke out hearts to prove to us, He only takes the best.*
....I really miss you Jay....:o(

Aaron Wdowin wrote at 2:58pm July 29th

Last Friday night at work I waited on a family of 4. The son had a bald head and was tall and thin. I didn't realize it might be cancer until I gave them the bill and saw that they all had been crying. They stayed at the table another hour just talking and every now and again they would all cry together. On their way out I stopped the kid (who was 21) and asked him if he was fighting cancer. He told me that he was diagnosed 2 months ago and that his family was out 'celebrating' his life. I told him about Lawrence, then I told him about you and I showed him the bracelets I wear on my wrist. I told him I wanted to give him my 'never quit' bracelet to help him fight through this...as I did my voice began to break. He said "it seems like it means a lot to you. Are you sure?" I said "yes" and put it on his wrist.

His family was nearby and his sister was tearing up as she listened. I hope it gives them all a little bit more hope and strength. I went back into the restaurant and it hit me. I had to go into the walk-in-cooler and I cried for 5 mins. I miss you bro. I miss you.
p.s. Jay a 5.8 earthquake just hit Chino, CA and rocked my house as I wrote this...you must be banging on your drums.

Eric Putrello wrote:

Remember the time at open jam at the Snubbing Post in Rome, with that crazy meth-head who was convinced that he was a drummer? He was trying to teach us a 'parallelogram' after we taught him how to do a paradiddle... or what if Dr. Seuss wrote a book of rudiments for drummers... flip flamaques and rip ratamaques. I love you, man and I miss you.

Gary Johnson wrote:

Hey man... probably the worst show we ever played was at the Kallet Theatre in Oneida in 2002... After the show, all 35 people that came to the 1000 capacity room came with us back to Denny's in Oneida, where the band proceeded to each take one of your drums out and make techno beats "Marching Band Style" while Mark threw glow sticks around in the parking lot.... It only got better when we went inside- when they wouldn't seat us in the Conference Room, I was dumb (and drunk

enough) to yell "It's because I'm black isn't it?" --
- not realizing that a guy who looked like The
Black Vin Diesel was standing right behind me.
Actually, I was about one intentional or
accidental-racial comment away from getting
lynched by the time that night was over... Our
waiter's nametag said "Dorkboy" and Amanda
Confer had Strawberry Milkshake fly out her nose
because you and Mark made her laugh so hard. It
was weird how we got thrown out... I totally didn't
see that coming....

So wait... that was the worst show we ever played...
but one time we scheduled a show at Champs with
60 Cycle Hum and about halfway through setup
we found out that they weren't letting 18 year olds
in. (60 Cycle Hum was used to ANGELS, where
the drinking age was 13.)Long story short --- we
tear down, start a phone tree and caravan... call up
our favorite dive bar Angels and say, "Hey, do you
guys want a band tonight?" The owner sounded
like a kid on Christmas when he said, "Oh shit.. I
need to go buy more beer." We packed about 300
people into a bar 25 miles away that night and
made about 300 bucks a guy. Not bad for a bunch
of teenagers.... and that was probably one of the
best shows we ever played.

I ran into Chuck Mikatin on Facebook one day. I
told him of this project and asked him if he would send me
a memory from their childhood. When I received this, I
immediately sent him an email grounding him to his room
for the entire weekend because I had never heard this one
before! I wonder if his wife enforced the grounding for me.

Chuck Mikatin wrote:

One time Jason and I were hunting groundhogs out back of his parent's house up on – blank- road and Jay thought a brilliant and exciting thing to do would be lighting the extremely dry and tall grass on fire. I informed Jay that this was actually a very bad and not well thought out plan, but Jason didn't heed my advice and proceeded to set even more grass aflame. At this point I decided to encourage him to cease his pyrotechnic escapade by threatening, or maybe actually shooting him with my air rifle. Jay laughed off my warning and kept on lighting. So I shot at him and he took off down a slope at the base of the hill, which we were upon. As I went to aim in order to fire another round upon my friend I heard a loud "Whoosh" and turned to see a sizable portion of wooden fencing on fire. I yelled at Jay and told him what he had done. We then ran to the house to find a bucket of water or some such piece of hi-tech fire fighting equipment with which we would be able to extinguish the flames.

Upon our return the blaze had spread to Biblical proportions and we nearly loosed our bowels and bladders in utter terror and despair. Somehow, with a few buckets of water, a blanket, one Airwalk shoe, and a little courage, we killed the raging inferno that had threatened to devour our beloved town of Camden. Upon that grassy knoll at the base of Wolcott Hill there could be seen for many years after our adventure a very black spot where the grass was never to grow again.

Chuck was in Jason's first band, Stone Soup. I always loved the name of that band. And, they were so young and cute! Steve Goodwill was also in that band. I didn't know how to get a hold of him after receiving this one, so I couldn't ground him!

Steve Goodwill wrote:
at 1:41pm on September 2nd, 2008

One time in 4th grade we had this substitute teacher and the lady who was subbing went out in the hall for whatever reason. Somehow…myself and some of the other students dared/convinced Jay to "go hide in the closet". Keep in mind, in elementary school the "closet" is simply one side of the room with hooks for jackets. Jay got up and hid in this closet with a jacket over him…only his eyes showing.

Sure enough, the teacher walks back in and continues teaching for maybe 20 minutes…oblivious to the emptiness of Jay's seat. The entire time I remember looking over at Jay who's face is about as red as a tomato with laughter…eyes tearing up. Finally our giggling and glancing over blew jays cover and the teacher is LIVID. We cracked up and all got in trouble of some sort. Even at that age… the kid was hysterical! Miss ya Jay.

Stone Soup 4ever!

I love it that they still send him messages as if he is here. I suppose he is still here in a way, because he is such a strong part of their memories.

180

I often hear people say (or post) that Jason sent them a "sign" – or they thank him for something they asked him for help with. It is strange, but there are several things that tell me he is always nearby as well.

Every night, when I am done at my office, I have nightly paperwork that has to be printed. Since probably the end of last summer, nearly every night when I submit the documents to print at the end of the night, I hear the "beep beep beep" of the printer being out of paper. There are two trays, and it does not matter if we are busy or slow, if we get out late, or even when I have had to do my paperwork in the morning for whatever reason. Every time I submit that job to print, the tray is out of paper.

At first, I would just get frustrated, because I had the fill the paper every night. Then, I suspected that my co-workers were just playing a trick on me, thinking it was funny. But, after determining that there wasn't anyone pranking me, my patient care representative, Heather, suggested one night that it was Jason messing with me. We laughed and said it would be just like him to do something like that.

But, after it continued to happen, I started to believe it was him, just saying – "Hey, Mom, I'm thinking about you!" It still happens to this day, nearly every night I close out. Now I am convinced it definitely is him, and every time I hear that "beep, beep, beep" I just smile and say "I know, Jas, I'm thinking about you, too!"

People still send requests to his MySpace and Facebook page to "add him as a friend," either because they change their page, or know someone he knew. When I get them, I always allow them to be added as friends, and it posts a message on the page that reads something like -

"Jason added **<name>** as a friend." Of course, it is usually a girl, since there were SO MANY gorgeous girls who knew and loved him. So, the kids still joke around with him. I thought this one was pretty funny…

Andy Sullivan wrote at 7:59pm December 7th
> *7 months later and Jay is still pickin' up women VIA online networking. I mean that guy was good!*

And they are creative in their memories…..

Cait LaLonde wrote:

> *This isn't really a story. It's just a poem and a little note that I wrote. Jay and I always used to joke around "Our Perfect Dream Lives" and I remember him saying one time completely joking around....You know Cait, one of these days, if I work hard enough, I'll be the man of your dreams.......at the time, I don't think either us were referring to the dreams when you are sleeping. However, either way, he was right!*

> *It's nights like tonight where I would call you when I couldn't sleep, because I knew you were tossing and turning, too.*

> *It's nights like tonight, I go to pick up my phone and get as far as calling you, just to have your voice mail remind me that you aren't able to answer.*

> *It's nights like tonight, I find comfort in hearing your voice, even if it's just a recording.*

> *It's nights like tonight when the song "Let It Be"*

will sing me to sleep.

It's nights like tonight where I do not cry tears of sadness, because you are not here.

It's nights like tonight, that when I close my eyes, I am happy.

Because...

It's in the dreams that I will dream tonight, I know you will be there with arms wide open ready to take me in.

&

It's the dreams that I dream tonight that give me comfort and support to be able to make it through without you here on Earth.

With these dreams like I dream tonight, you have taught me to never stop dreaming, because it is then where you will actually answer, and that is when all of my wishes really do come true.

Jason Christopher,
    Thank you for everything that you have taught me, whether it was on purpose or by mistake, whether it was loud and clear when you were here or whether it's been from the breath of an angel and whispered in the wind. I respect it all and keep it very close to my heart. I miss you, my dear friend. Happy Birthday, Merry Christmas, and Happy New Year. I love you till the end of time. Until we meet again....please keep coming to me in my dreams.

Love Always,
Cait

Bob Fleming became Jason's step father when he
was 7. On January 20th, he sent me this message.

> *As I write this on Inauguration Day it
> reminds me of several things about Jason. I wish
> so much he could be here this day to see history
> unfold. I am sure he is in heaven smiling this
> morning.*

> *Many times when Jay was growing up we
> discussed how racist many people are and how
> senseless and unfair it is to be that way. Treating
> people as equals no matter what race they happen
> to be is something that has always been important
> to me. I have always hoped all my kids would be
> like me in that regard and I am proud to say that I
> think they are.*

> *One morning I happened to see something
> on his drum set that made me so very proud of
> him. I don't know where he got it but will never
> forget the feeling of pride I got when I saw it. It
> was a simple sticker that he saw fit to stick on the
> bass drum. It read "Racism Sucks!"*

> *On a lighter note, I remember a time we
> were driving someplace. Jay was in the back seat
> and started cracking Polish jokes, laughing his
> head off at each one. I didn't say anything at first
> and let him tell a few more. I'll never forget the
> look on his face and the silence when I said to
> him, "I don't know what you find so funny, Jason.*

Do you know that you're part polish? Your mom's last name was Closinski. I never again heard another ethnic joke from him.

Another of my favorite memories was on another drive. A family of ducks was crossing the road and a car ahead of us hit them. After we passed them Jason looked out the back window and I heard him say, "Gee why did he have to hit them all?"
So may cherished memories. I am fortunate that I was a part of his life. He was a remarkable young man. I am quite certain Heaven is a better place with him there and the Angel Band sounds so much better with JayCW behind the drums!

*****

So, one of the inspirations for the 'resurrection' of the birth of this book was the memorial service we had in November, when Jason's headstone was put in. Andy and I had designed the stone, and we took our time to make sure it was exactly as we wanted it, since I had to stare at it every time I went up to see him. We chose a portrait picture of him from Bob and Chrissy Scales' wedding that showed how incredibly handsome he was, and how nice he "cleaned up". Then in the center of the stone, we had the rim of a snare drum carved, and a picture of him rocking out on his drums in the center of it. On the back, we had the second verse of "Let It Be" inscribed. Almost.

The monument company sends out proofs of the stone, exactly as they are going to carve it. When you get the proof, you have to sign off on the accuracy, or change anything that needs to be changed. The words on the back page were not right in the proof. We typed up what needed to be corrected, and sent it back in with notes from the

185

owner of the company. The stone came in about five or six weeks later - with the same mistake on the back. It should have read:

> "And when the broken hearted people
> Living in the world agree…"

However, the first line was not correct. It actually reads:

> "And when the broken hearted people
> In the world would agree….."

Now, if you recall, I mentioned earlier how little tolerance Jason had for people who could not do their jobs correctly. I asked everyone at the memorial service if they had noticed, and if they heard the resounding scream from Jason asking if "ANYONE in his whole life could do their job without screwing up!"

I was talking with my sister about what I was going to do about the error. She said, "I would leave it like it is just to bug him!" I may just do that.

Wayne Clemens did get to "officiate" at the memorial service in November, and did a wonderful job. I had just meant for it to be a "little get together" for Jason's close friends, and family to get together to see the stone, and to help in the healing process. Some of the kids were still having such a hard time. I kept his phone turned on, and he was still getting regular txt messages and voicemails from them all. They were still so raw emotionally, I thought the service would allow them to get to the next level in the healing process.

I think there were about 50 people there that day. It

was rainy and chilly, but they didn't care. They all came out to see the stone and to be together again. They told stories and that is what motivated me to resurrect the idea for this book. I didn't have Jason to help me to remember the stories about him, but everyone there had something to offer. I just had to ask.

It's been almost eight months since Jason passed as I am writing this. I still cry at least once every day, sometimes from a song that reminds me, sometimes from a sudden thought that he is really still gone, sometimes because I think of calling him to ask him something, or get his opinion on some random thought. I guess most days, it is easier than it was, but still mind-boggling because it is so "out of order" of what we perceive to be natural.

.   And the memories keep coming, and I hope he will continue to inspire his friends and family, and we keep his spirit alive forever.

*****

My sister and brothers set up the JASON CHRISTOPHER WILHELM SCHOLARSHIP FUND. It is a charity fund to give scholarships to Camden music or sports students for college. It is also designed to make donations to Cancer related causes, or people and families affected by this dreaded disease. I know Jason and I had talked about something like that when he was here, and apparently, he had talked to some of his friends about it as well, as Bob Scales mentioned in his hunting story. I am hoping that any proceeds from this book will add to the fund, as well as annual fundraisers we are setting up. We are planning on having the May party every year for people who knew and loved him to be able to all get together, celebrate his memory and their friendships, and raise money for the fund.

www.jaycwsfund.org

Let It Be
Lennon/McCartney

When I find myself in times of trouble
Mother Mary comes to me
Speaking words of wisdom
Let it be.
And in my hour of darkness
She is standing right in front of me
Speaking words of wisdom
Let it be.

Let it be, let it be, let it be yeah, let it be
Whisper words of wisdom
Let it be.

And when the broken hearted people
Living in the world agree
There will be an answer
Let it be.
For though thcy may be parted
There is still a chance
That they will see
There will be an answer
Let it be.

And when the night is cloudy
There is still a light that shines on me
Shine until tomorrow
Let it be.
I wake up to the sound of music
Mother Mary comes to me
Speaking words of wisdom
Let it be.

My Jason Story:

.

.

.

My Jason Story:

My Jason Story: